To G

LET'S TALK ABOUT

FAITH AND INTELLECT

From Mike & Carolyn

OTHER BOOKS IN THE
LET'S TALK ABOUT SERIES

Let's Talk about Polygamy

Let's Talk about Religion and Mental Health

Let's Talk about the Book of Abraham

Let's Talk about the Law of Consecration

*Let's Talk about the Translation of
the Book of Mormon (coming early 2023)*

For more information on the other books
in the Let's Talk About series,
visit DesBook.com/LetsTalk.

LET'S TALK ABOUT

FAITH AND INTELLECT

TERRYL GIVENS

SALT LAKE CITY, UTAH

All images are in the public domain, unless noted otherwise.

© 2022 Terryl L. Givens

All rights reserved. No part of this book may be reproduced in any form or by any means without permission in writing from the publisher, Deseret Book Company, at permissions@deseretbook.com. This work is not an official publication of The Church of Jesus Christ of Latter-day Saints. The views expressed herein are the responsibility of the author and do not necessarily represent the position of the Church or of Deseret Book Company.

DESERET BOOK is a registered trademark of Deseret Book Company.

Visit us at deseretbook.com

Library of Congress Cataloging-in-Publication Data
(CIP data on file)
ISBN 978-1-63993-041-8

Printed in the United States of America
PubLitho, Draper, UT

10 9 8 7 6 5 4 3 2 1

To the fellowship:

Ryan, Dan, Morgan, George, Thomas, Fred, Steve, Bill, and Phil.

Models all.

CONTENTS

Introduction 1

SECTION I: PROLOGUE

1. Myths and Straw Men: Reason and Christian Beginnings 17

2. Inquisitions and Intellect in Christian History 24

SECTION II: RESTORATION

3. Heart and Mind United 33

4. The Problem of God, Good, and Evil 48

5. The Stories We Tell 55

6. Scripture 70

7. The "New Mormon History" 84

8. The Poverty of Secularism 92

Conclusion 98

Epilogue 108

Further Reading 111

Notes 114

Index 129

INTRODUCTION

> "Faith and the quest for knowledge
> are not inconsistent; they are
> compatible and complementary."
> —Elder Quentin L. Cook

It has been said that when it comes to the news media, you have two choices. You can ignore it and be uninformed. Or you can pay attention and be misinformed.[1] This is particularly true when it comes to the status of religious faith in our present cultural moment. One would think from news reports that religious belief is at an all-time low. What is true is that institutional *affiliation* is dropping off precipitously, while popular *attacks* on religion are *rising* precipitously. These include both "government restrictions on religion and social hostilities."[2] However, increasing alienation from institutional forms of religion does not say a great deal about what's going on in the hearts and minds of those searching for a personal faith in God; and the desperate quality of today's vocal atheists may suggest that some doubters are feeling a crisis of doubt as much as the believers are confronting a crisis of faith.[3]

In American culture, at any rate, the persistence of faith is not limited to isolated enclaves of the undereducated. Over the last century, more than 60 percent of Nobel laureates have been Christian.[4] In 1969, the Carnegie Commission surveyed over sixty thousand American academics on their religious commitments. *Over* 50 percent of mathematicians, physical scientists, life scientists, economists, and political scientists identified themselves as "religious." And in the past decade? A 2014 survey conducted by the *Economist* determined that, in America at least, "scientists are only a bit less religious than the average American."⁵ In a subsequent study, only one-third of US scientists thought the science-religion relationship was one of conflict.⁶ In 2018, an astronomer observed that "the apparent conflict between science and religion is a relatively recent phenomenon, that's been 'invigorated' by the media's need for drama."⁷ In philosophy departments, trends of the last decades have been so favorable to belief in God that some secularists are alarmed. "Almost overnight," one complains, "it became . . . 'academically respectable' to argue for theism."⁸

What about Latter-day Saints in particular? Can any generalizations be drawn about intellect and faith, or education and religious observance in the Church of Jesus Christ? At the turn of the present century, one important study revealed that members of the Church—in the United States, where the social science data are available—are an exception to the widely held secularization hypothesis (the view that links "secularization"—and its emphasis on scientific, rational thought—with a decline in religion). This study found, contrary to the general pattern, that for Latter-day Saint men and women, "the *higher* the level of education, the *higher* one's level of religious observance."⁹

Clearly, educated, thoughtful, reasonable people can and do find a comfortable synthesis between the life of the mind and the life of faith. Equally obvious is the fact that many people are not finding the two compatible. Many intellectual challenges to faith have existed from the earliest days of the Christian tradition—and they will always continue. Christianity was predicated on the seemingly absurd claim that a man crucified and then buried in a tomb for three days rose from the dead and ascended to heaven. That story took hold and flourished in a Roman society that had inherited the richest philosophical traditions in the Western world. Even the Apostles themselves were initially incredulous of the Resurrection, dismissing the report of Mary out of hand: "Now when Jesus was arisen early the first day of the week, he appeared first to Mary Magdalene, out of whom he had cast seven devils. And she went and told them that had been with him, as they mourned and wept. And they, when they had heard that he was alive, and had been seen of her, believed not" (Mark 16:9–11).[10] Then, as now, believers had to contend with common sense, lived experience, the tragedy and finality of death, and the demands of reason. Then, as now, one did not find a durable faith by ignoring those demands, but by acknowledging that in all of life's most important transactions and commitments and decisions, we rely upon a broad array of resources to find our way through the darkness.

Reason has its strengths. So do experience, conscience, intuition, emotion, and other inner faculties that may have other names or no name. All these resources may constitute the basis of a faith that is solidly rooted on evidence that is "real . . . because it is discernible" (Alma 32:35). That is my thesis in this book. My twin emphases will be on those ways in which reason and intellect sustain belief in those propositions held by believing members of The Church of Jesus Christ of Latter-day Saints, and on those moments or areas where the historical and personal resources of intellect are not adequate to fully address matters of deepest import. In other words, faith is sustained by intellect, and where intellect falls short, additional resources available to us provide a valid basis for commitment to Christ and His gospel.

This is *not* to say that our brains get us only so far along the road to understanding and wisdom, at which point we must stop short before the unsearchability of the deepest truths and simply succumb to the mystery. Faith is not just a hopeful leap into the dark, wishful thinking against the grain of the evidence. The thoughtful, reflective faith of which I will be writing considers the findings of science, the lessons of history, the insights of philosophy, and the best reasonings of our intellect. And it *adds to those* an openness to other faculties, a receptivity to the intimations of the heart, confidence in the moral intuitions of the soul, and forms of trusting and knowing for which we may not even have language.

We may be embodied brains, supersophisticated computing systems in an environment of pulsing flesh. And we are doubtless biological organisms, with a history of competition in the trial of life, struggling for survival and reproducibility. However, there is more to be said on the subject of human identity. We are complex beings, and our nature is not reducible to a few drives and appetites. The psychologist Abraham Maslow changed the field of modern psychology when he went beyond simplistic Darwinian models of human motivation to place, at the top of his hierarchy of human needs, "self-actualization." Jonathan Haidt extends this key to human nature by invoking what he identifies as a universal human impulse "to find the staircase amid all the clutter." In his experience as a teacher and social scientist, people are "all searching for the staircase," bearing witness to the human drive and the capacity for "self-transcendence."[11] Yes, we crave food and drink. We want physical comforts and respond to sexual motivations. As biological beings, our bodily needs demand our attention and satisfaction. Maslow's breakthrough question (like that of Haidt) was the implied, "And then?" That is the question with undeniable resonance—one that reason and faith combine most compellingly to answer.

Maslow's conception behind the principle of "self-actualization" moves us in the direction of what is most distinctly human. He writes, "Even if all these [primary, basic] needs are satisfied, . . . a new discontent and restlessness will soon develop, unless the individual is doing what he is fitted for. A musician must make music, an artist must paint, a poet must write, if he is to be ultimately happy. What a man can be, he must be. This need we may call self-actualization."[12]

Doing what we are fitted for. *What humans can be, they must be*. One might suspect Maslow of a latent religious agenda, but he is talking about how we experience life itself, not abstract

INTRODUCTION *bears*

spirituality or dogmas. He is describing our nagging sense that stasis and contentment are not consistent with our deepest drives or identity. We have needs and aspirations that go far beyond any strictly biological program. This strikes me as a first glimpse of a reasonable basis for faith: we are constituted such that materialistic analyses of our human condition highlight the very things they cannot satisfactorily explain. One is reminded here of the great psychologist David Premack, who lamented, "Why is it that the biologist E. O. Wilson can spot the difference between two kinds of ants at a hundred yards, but he can't see the difference between an ant and a human?"[13]

For most of human history the demands of simple survival made the practical necessities of life paramount. In our contemporary moment in the first world, affluence has shifted our attention from what is meaningful to what is distracting. When Thomas Merton, the great Trappist monk, was asked to diagnose the "leading spiritual disease of our time," he responded unexpectedly, "Efficiency."[14] That's a curious verdict. Why would faster computers, work-saving apps, more compact cellphones, and higher-speed internet be implicated in spiritual illness? Perhaps because in our euphoria to get from A to B more quickly, we have forgotten to ask how worthwhile the destination is. The greater our velocity, the more efficient our journey, the fewer the pauses along the way to take stock and survey the scenery, to ask questions and to listen. To ponder and reflect and live more deeply. It all reminds one of the poet William Wordsworth; excited to be making his first trek across the Alps, he bustled along the path for days. When he stopped to ask for directions through the last pass, he learned he had already made the crossing. It was a few miles behind him—but he had been oblivious to the experience while it unfolded. His journey had been quick and efficient—but he had missed the moment.

Hugh Nibley weaves the modern parable of a successful businessman who suddenly learns that he has mere weeks to live.

LET'S TALK ABOUT FAITH AND INTELLECT

In the days that follow, this man's thinking undergoes a . . . quick and brutal reorientation. . . . Things that once filled him with awe seem strangely trivial, and things which a few days before did not even exist for him now fill his consciousness. For the first time he discovers the . . . beauty of the world of nature. . . . The perfection of children comes to him like a sudden revelation. . . . Everywhere he looks he gets the feeling that all is passing away. . . . He sees all life and stuff about him involved in a huge ceaseless combustion, a literal and apparent process of oxidation which is turning some things slowly, some rapidly, but all things surely to ashes. . . .

'What has happened to our solid citizen?' his friends ask perplexed. He has chosen to keep his disease a secret, . . . [but] he cannot conceal his change of heart. As far as his old associates can see, the poor man has left the world of reality. . . .

Now the question arises, has this man been jerked out of reality or into it?[15]

To ask, "Are we moving toward or away from the deepest reality we are capable of recognizing?" is to pause on this side of the pass through the mountains, rather than the other.

Let's be clear what this parable is *not* saying. It is not asking, "Are we ready to face God? Have we procrastinated our repentance too late?" In fact, the point of the story is not religious in the conventional way. "Depend upon it, sir, when a man knows he is to be hanged in a fortnight, it concentrates his mind wonderfully," said Samuel Johnson. In light of Maslow's insight, the concentrated mind might, in the most general sense, turn to the simple questions: Have I done what I was fitted for? What I could be, have I become? Have I lived, in other words, in accordance with the highest aspirations of my nature? It doesn't take a philosopher, a theologian, or a psychologist to tell us what we have all experienced: We yearn to love and be loved. We yearn to know. And our nature is fitted for both. As the playwright Tom Stoppard wrote: "It's wanting to know that makes us matter. Otherwise we're going out the way we came in."[16]

The need to love and be loved is acute, it is constant, and it does not diminish with age. My focus at present is on the second of those higher needs: the human compulsion to know, to understand, to discern. This compulsion is an irresistible invitation to a life in which we nourish the intellect and its fruits, supplemented by a faith that can open to our understanding unseen worlds of truth and goodness and beauty. This is the kind of life that scripture refers to as a pursuit of "learning even by study and also by faith" (Doctrine and Covenants 109:7).

The seeds of this hunger are planted deep within us and are universal. Aristotle observed that we all, by nature, "desire to know."[17] Some fine distinctions are necessary here. The great humanitarian Lowell Bennion wrote that "love of knowing, without the love of learning, leads to dissipation of the mind."[18] In other words, it is not the satisfaction or complacency of knowing as much as the passion and drive of *wanting to know* that is elevating and ennobling; the first may simply gratify pride or ambition; the second is the motive force behind growth, discovery, and life in its abundance and variety.

One eighteenth-century philosopher wrote that "the first and the simplest emotion which we discover in the human mind is curiosity."[19] And curiosity knows no fetters. From childhood, we have pondered the mysteries of our world. Why is snow white, but rain clear? And where does the color go when it melts? Later we may ask how a monarch butterfly navigates a journey of three thousand miles, or a salmon finds its way back to its home waters after a journey of twice that distance. We may wonder how the eye turns electromagnetic waves into the iridescence of the dragonfly's wings, or the nose transforms differing flights of molecules into the fragrance of baked bread or of a baby's breath. However, once we come to a certain age, our native curiosity—once as raw and disparate as a gushing stream—of necessity funnels into one rivulet out of hundreds; a major or trade is chosen, and our focused study narrows. With employment, our preoccupations are further reduced, and before long our mental energies—called to life's other tasks—fall into alignment with career responsibilities, long-term objectives, and the routine of life.

Meanwhile, other forces work to dim our curiosity about questions of ultimate meaning.

With the undifferentiating instinct of that first innocence, I may ask why my father suffered a painful passing from cancer, if I lived before this life, or if another sun will rise in a different dawn after my own death. However, in a world where, for the first time in Western history, faith in God appears as one choice among many respectable options (Charles Taylor's famous definition of this "secular age" [20]), religious questions carry new baggage. A considerable number of public figures, popular writers, academics, and intellectuals maintain with particular vehemence that religious questions are unanswerable at best and irrational or absurd at worst. The volume of these voices is such that Latter-day Saints may reasonably and understandably ask, Is there a place in our faith tradition for individuals who want to remain passionately committed to the life of the mind *and* the demands of rational thought? Is there, in the simplest terms, a possible harmony between faith and intellect, religion and reason?

As framed, these questions are a misdirection. To segregate forms and ways of knowing into the religious and the intellectual, though a common practice from the earliest ages, is fraught with misdirection—mostly because our yearning to know does not organize itself neatly into such categories. To cite Maslow once more, "Even after we know, we are impelled to know more and more minutely and microscopically on the one hand, and on the other, more and more extensively in the direction of a world philosophy, religion."[21] Of course the scientific method is different than a Euclidean proof, which is different than a meta-analysis in psychology, which is different than Alma's methodology for ascertaining truth. *Knowing* that

God lives (or kindred assertions) is subject to different modes of ultimate verification than other forms of truth claims in other fields of human investigation. But that doesn't place them outside of rational activity.

The Restoration tradition at its best not only accommodates but promotes and invites rigorous thought, sustained inquiry, and tough questions. Intellect and reason enrich our faith, and our faith reinforces and supplements our intellect. As G. K. Chesterton observed, "The madman is not the man who has lost his reason. The madman is the man who has lost everything except his reason."[22] Knowledge by itself makes for a sterile existence. It is our freedom to shape a future as a *response* to what we know constitutes whatever good we create—or cocreate—in life. A cow awakes hungry, and then it grazes in the field. There is a linear, invariable line between its present knowledge (I am hungry) and whatever future unfolds (I eat). But I, the human, may awake hungry and instead of eating, I may paint the *Mona Lisa*. Or serve in a Calcutta slum. Or I might just buy a glazed donut. What makes me different from a bovine creature in the most significant regard is that my knowledge unfolds within a field of meaning and values and beliefs.

I can *choose* the future that I will, at least in part, constitute. I could possess all the information of all the world's combined data centers, beholding the inputs from a million cameras. But to observe, to register, to know, are of themselves sterile. Pure knowledge, shorn of any bridge to acting upon the world, gets us no closer to *doing* and *being* what we are fitted for. Faith has many shades of meaning in the context of what follows, but we may generally understand faith as confidence in a frame of ultimate values that beckon us beyond the satisfactions of immediate needs. Or we could say with Chesterton that religious faith is "a real trust in some external standard as a reality."[23] And I will be asserting that Restoration teachings invite our rational assent to, trust in, and engagement with the reality they depict. And that the God they invite us to know, and the story they tell about our origins and destiny, provide a morally and intellectually compelling framework that explains—and nourishes—our hunger to know.

Reason, then, like reflection, evidence, and thoughtful contemplation, operates jointly with our embrace and enactment of ultimate values and truths—and, as we will see, with the particular propositions of the Restoration. We are *fitted* to ask questions about the origin of the cosmos and of the human soul; we are *fitted* to ponder when the sun will exhaust itself in the long process of nuclear fusion; and we are *fitted* to consider whether my love for friends and parents will with time similarly fade into nothing more than spent atoms. We are children of wonder, fueled by curiosity from birth to death's door, and we are clearly fitted to make progress in understanding both the minute and the majestic. "Curiosity and poor eyesight" fuel the quest, noted one perceptive writer.[24]

Astonishingly, not only our own spiritual makeup but also the physical world we inhabit is uniquely configured to assist us in that task of understanding. The God behind the workings of all that is visible clearly intends that we understand His physical handiwork. The poet John Milton may have believed that we should "be lowly wise: Think only what concerns thee and thy being; [and] Dream not of other Worlds,"[25] but our home planet appears, in crucial regards, to be designed like an observatory that provides us a front-row seat to penetrate the mysteries of this and "other Worlds."

Two examples of many stand out: earthlings have the unique advantage of living on a planet from which a large moon has the virtually identical apparent diameter as the sun—an extraordinarily rare scenario in planetary systems. During a total eclipse, the moon completely and exactly occludes the disc of the sun, while allowing us to observe its full corona. Observations on these carefully timed occasions have been instrumental in the development of spectroscopy, a field that not only allows us to understand the composition of and processes occurring in the sun but has also led to the development of stellar astrophysics. In sum, perfect solar eclipses "have helped reveal the nature of stars, provided a natural experiment for testing Einstein's General Theory of Relativity, and allowed us to measure the slowdown of Earth's rotation."[26]

A second example is the set of conditions that makes distant cosmic observations possible: an unusually transparent atmosphere, a stable planetary rotation, our precise position within the galaxy (beneath the plane of a galactic arm, with clear lines of sight), and the relative isolation of the Milky Way itself. These conditions all optimize our opportunities to observe, measure, and understand the diverse structures and composition of the universe. As one astronomer writes, "We occupy the best overall place for observation in the Milky Way galaxy which is itself the best type of galaxy to learn about stars, galactic structure, and the distant universe simultaneously."[27]

Other writers note the remarkable cosmic *timing* of our day for knowledge growth. Lawrence Krauss writes in *A Universe from Nothing*, "Observers in the far future will see . . . a single galaxy housing their star and their planet surrounded by an otherwise vast, empty, static space." In a rather stunning repudiation of the idea that there is nothing special about the time or place in which humanity finds itself in the wider universe, Krauss comments that it is a "strange coincidence" that we live in this unique window of time where the after-effects of the Big Bang are still perceptible.[28] Marcelo Gleiser writes: "Those unfortunate cosmologists of the future, if basing their science only on what they could measure, would construct an erroneous picture of the world, missing the fact that their bleak predicament has an explanation tracing back trillions of years into the past. Their static cosmos would be an illusion, a consequence of their living within a cosmological horizon where galaxies don't follow an expansionary trend, as they do in ours."[29]

These and other conditions about planet Earth are uniquely constituted to satisfy our yearning to see and understand the

Figure 1. The Tarantula Nebula

cosmos we inhabit. As Einstein marveled, "The eternal mystery of the world is its comprehensibility. . . . The fact that it is comprehensible is a miracle."[30] The God behind the Creation is evidently a God who delights to reveal and divulge, to enhance our growth and feed our minds as well as our souls. We may well ask, "Has Christianity always seen God in such terms? Have we as Latter-day Saints?" The record is mixed.

In what follows, I will briefly trace by way of prologue the place of reason and intellect in the Christian past, from the Hebrew Bible through the Reformation. In section II, I will discuss the Restoration as inviting a unity of heart and mind, of faith and intellect. In that section, we will see how the Church of Jesus Christ engages the great questions surrounding God, the nature of evil and suffering, and our place in the universe. I will in subsequent chapters address some of those challenges that have arisen to our confidence in scripture, and our narratives about the Restoration. Does it provide a rationally compelling framework for addressing the most pressing questions of ultimate meaning? And we will confront the question, Is an abiding faith in the face of secularism's challenges reasonable and sustainable? The result of our journey will affirm two facts. "Our intellect can feed our spirit, and our spirit can feed our intellect," as the Apostle Joseph B. Wirthlin recognized.[31] And in Elder Neal A. Maxwell's words, "How intellectually amazing the gospel of Jesus Christ is!"[32]

uniquely eclectic

SECTION I
PROLOGUE

Pre-christianity? (handwritten)

CHAPTER 1

MYTHS AND STRAW MEN: REASON AND CHRISTIAN BEGINNINGS

> *From the first Christian centuries, Christian writers saw faith and reason as complementary, not opposed. Tertullian's famous "I believe because it is absurd" makes good copy, but it is more folklore than fact.*

The most anguished character in the Bible is the suffering Job. His harrowing physical torments and the emotional agony of losing his family hardly register in the narrative against the backdrop of a greater pain: incomprehension in the face of mortality's tragic unfolding. Again and again, Job struggles to make rational sense of his predicament. He knows he has been righteous. He knows God is just. And he knows he is suffering unjustly. Nothing adds up. "How . . . shall I . . . choose out my words and reason with him?" he exclaims. "I desire to reason with God," he declares a few chapters later. "Hear now my reasoning," he pleads, wanting to understand and be understood. Meanwhile, his friend Eliphaz rebukes him for trying to make sense of it all. "Should a wise man . . . reason with unprofitable talk?" Yet Job persists stubbornly, trusting that a loving God would be typified more by reasonableness than by sheer power: "an upright person could reason with him," he insists (Job 9:14; 13:3; 13:6; 15:3; 23:7, NRSV).

In the end, Job's impulses and his confidence are rewarded. When the Lord makes Himself known, Job implores Him directly. "Hear, and I will speak. I will question you, and you declare to me" (Job 42:4, NRSV). His friends, who had counseled Job to abjectly submit to God's inscrutable will, are chastised ("Ye have not spoken of me the thing that is right" [42:7]). Job, while chastened for his premature conclusions, is blessed for his steadfast quest for understanding. This may be one of the Bible's most important lessons. In this, the most soul-stretching book of scripture, we are confronted with the universal struggle to find clarity amid the darkness, enlightenment to steer us through the innocence into which we are born. Job struggles valiantly, even defiantly, while his companions indulge in trite explanations ("Man is born unto trouble" [5:7]), facile blaming ("Whoever perished, being innocent?" [4:7]), or contented ignorance ("We are but of yesterday, and know nothing" [8:9]). Critics have long pointed out that God's answer out of the whirlwind hardly seems like the explanation Job was seeking. But as the great biblical scholar Robert Alter notes, "The moment the Voice begins to address Job out of the storm, Job already has his answer: that, despite appearances to the contrary, God cares enough about man to reveal Himself to humankind."[1] And indeed, Job reaps a rich harvest of ignorance dispelled and mythologies exploded.[2]

One legacy of the Hebrew Bible is a Jewish culture devoted to the interconnection of religion and learning. "Come, let us reason together," is an invitation that generations of Jews have taken to heart with a passion. More controversial has been the place of the intellect in Christian understanding. It has become popular in some circles today to associate Christianity with anti-intellectualism, or at least to assert the incompatibility of faith and reason.

On the topic of religious faith and intellect generally, the waters are muddied in public discourse because even respectable figures in both speech and in print poison the well by defining "faith" in terms few Christians would accept. "Belief" that has "no connection with evidence," claims one;[3] "a process that bypasses any need for evidence" echoes another.[4] Even standard internet sources spout such silliness: "Faith is the belief in the truth of something that does not

Figure 2. The Complaint of Job, by William Blake

require any evidence," asserts one.⁵ Such critics like to cite the damning words of the Christian church father Tertullian (AD 160–230): *creo quia absurdum est,* or, "I believe because it is absurd."⁶ The problem is, Tertullian never uttered those words. Rather, like George Washington cutting down the cherry tree, the meme and its false attribution infiltrated popular culture long after Tertullian's death and continues in force to the present.

Like many myths, there is a grain of truth behind the story, but the richness and complexity of the subject is lost in the human preference for simple dichotomies and formulations that one may either embrace mindlessly or dismiss out of hand. Tertullian did write something vaguely similar, an ironic comment about the failure of the Christ story to conform to reasonable standards: "It is [*credibile*, or believable] because it is [*ineptum*, or unfitting]; . . . the fact is certain because it is impossible."⁷ He was actually making an argument similar to the one pronounced by Aristotle centuries earlier, when the philosopher explained that "the apparent incredibility of a reported claim can actually provide a reason for believing it, since a witness seeking to perpetuate a false story would most likely have come up with something that at least seemed plausible."[8] So Tertullian was not equating faith with nonsense. He was saying that if you wanted to attract disciples to a new religion that you had invented out of whole cloth, you would not base it on an event that is readily dismissed as fantasy. So claiming such an unlikely event as a resurrection actually suggests it was not pure invention—or so goes the logic of Aristotle and Tertullian.

As is evident in his writings, Tertullian was himself of two minds about the relationship of faith to reason. On the one hand, he taught that "nothing ought to be believed hastily" or "without examination" and that God is "the author of reason."[9] At the same time, unaided reason, he was convinced, could never provide those answers that faith alone could give us. And so, he asked in his second-most quoted formulation, *"What indeed has Athens to do with Jerusalem?"*[10] With those words, Tertullian posed the question that continues to engage millions today. How do we accommodate our respect for intellect and reason on the one hand ("Athens," the home of Western philosophy) and religious faith on the other ("Jerusalem," first home of the Christian church)? Tertullian's formulation was a rhetorical question; he implied the two were self-evidently separate and distinct areas.

Today, many moderns make the same point by calling science and religion "non-overlapping magisteria," domains that ask different questions and employ different methods. As formulated by Stephen Jay Gould, "No such conflict should exist because each subject has a legitimate magisterium, or domain of teaching authority. . . . The net of science covers the empirical universe: what is it made of (fact) and why does it work this way (theory). The net of religion extends over questions of moral meaning and value. These two magisteria do not overlap."[11] Safely insulated from each other, the thinking goes, intellectuals can pursue objective truth about reality, while the religious can ask their own questions and find their own answers unimpeded by the constraints of either reason or evidence.

Nonetheless, it is in fact the case that some Christians have pushed their distrust for human reason so far that reason has no place alongside faith. Those Christians who agree that reason contributes little or nothing to the life of faith are called *fideists*. "Their position," notes Étienne Gilson, "is very simple. Since God has spoken to us, it is no longer necessary for us to think."[12] They latched on rather too literally to Paul's comment that "the wisdom of the world is evil and foolishness a good thing" (1 Corinthians 1:25–26)—as did mockers of Christianity in those first Christian centuries.[13] Paul, however, did not mean his words to the Corinthians as a rebuke to those who believed that reason could itself be godly and good. In fact, when Paul is challenged by the philosophers of Athens (Epicureans and Stoics), he applauded them as "god-fearing," or "extremely religious" (not "too superstitious," as Protestant translators pejoratively rendered δεισιδαιμονεστερος [Acts 17:22]). The plain fact is that Paul as well as the church fathers were deeply influenced by the Greek intellectual tradition and assimilated their methods, tools, and often their values and ideas.

Other early Christian fathers were outspoken in defending the value of human reason and the Greek intellectual tradition in particular. The Christian apologist Justin Martyr (100–165) was enormously appreciative of the contributions of the Greek philosophers and even wore the gallium (the philosopher's cloak) in tribute to them. He recognized their greatness, saw their philosophy as preparation for the gospel, and went so far as to declare that "Christ . . . was the divine Word or logos which had enlightened thinkers like Socrates." Many such enlightened pagans, he wrote, "were unconscious Christians."[14]

Tertullian's own contemporary Clement of Alexandria affirmed the opinion of Justin. He wrote that "we shall not err in alleging that . . . philosophy more especially was given to the Greeks, as a covenant peculiar to them." Such learning "is a stepping-stone to the philosophy which is according to Christ."[15] As one historian notes, "We owe it above all to him [Clement] if scholarly thinking and research are recognized in the Church. He proved that faith and philosophy [philosophia—love of wisdom], Gospel and secular learning, are not enemies but belong together."[16]

While Jerusalem did little to marginalize philosophy in the first century, Rome itself did. Little remarked upon in the history of anti-intellectualism is the fact that it was in the Roman empire, not the Christian, that philosophy was first exiled. Under Nero (who ruled AD 54–68), philosophical books were burned, and their authors (mostly Stoics and Cynics) were exiled and executed. The victims were condemned as "stubborn and rebellious persons, contemptuous of magistrates and kings." Vespasian, Nero's successor, "expelled from Rome all the philosophers" with only one exception. Their offense was "teach[ing] doctrines inappropriate to the time." Titus, ruling circa AD 80, followed suit, as did Domitian, who in 94 executed Arulenus Rusticus for no greater crime than "because he was a philosopher."[17]

The first systematic expounder of a Christian theology was the third-century father Origen of Alexandria. His master work, *First Principles*, was the most important systematic treatment of Christian teaching in the church's first centuries. And his words regarding the relationship between faith and intellect resonate through the years:

> Beyond all comparison does the mind burn with an inexpressible desire to know the reason of those things which we see done by God This desire this longing, we believe to be unquestionably implanted within us by God; and as the eye naturally seeks the light and vision and our body naturally desires food and drink so our mind is possessed with a becoming and natural desire to become acquainted with the truth of God and the causes of things. Now we have received this desire from God, not in order that it should never be gratified or be *capable* of gratification. Otherwise

the love of truth would appear to have been implanted by God into our minds to no purpose.

Furthermore, he adds, those whose "minds are directed to the study and love the investigation of truth, are . . . made fitter for receiving the instruction that is to come."[18]

In the nineteenth century, at the dawn of what one might call a "modern religious sensibility," Friedrich Schleiermacher defined religion with historic, lasting impact. Religion, said he, is a "sense and taste for the Infinite." Feeling, he insisted, "lies at the heart of all genuine religious experience."[19] From this point on, a growing public conceived of religion as emotion-centered, as interior experience, as subjective truth. Certainly, religion deals with suprasensory realities, and undoubtedly faith itself presupposes ways of knowing that transcend or supplement the tactile and the rational. The danger, and one that has widely come to pass, is the reduction of religion to emotion, to feeling alone. Influential Christians like Origen knew better. And so should Latter-day Saints.

CHAPTER 2

INQUISITIONS AND INTELLECT IN CHRISTIAN HISTORY

Nonbelievers have a field day rehearsing the story of Galileo and the church's persecution of scientists. In actual fact, the Galileo story is complicated, and his silencing by the church an outlier. The Western church invented the university, encouraged learning, and provided the main agents behind the intellectual revolutions of the post-Enlightenment world.

Once the Christian church became a dominant institution in Western civilization, did it foster or did it stifle intellectual freedom and the growth of human knowledge? Christian history, in this regard, echoes the "love-hate relationship between philosophy and faith that has gone on for close on two thousand years," in one writer's words.[1] On balance the record strongly supports the faith's positive impact on Western intellectual history. The advances for which the church was responsible were far more profound and lasting than the setbacks that occurred from time to time.

Mythologies with little basis in fact are slow to fade. The "Dark Ages" was a pejorative term introduced by a devotee of classicism who lamented the passing of Rome's empire. Scholars today reject the term, with one historian arguing the Middle Ages should actually be called the "light ages" because of the progress of intellectual culture.[2] The exaggerated "warfare between science and theology" was largely an invention of nineteenth-century writers like John Draper and A. D. White, caught up in the secular biases and enthusiasm of their age. As one example of the latter's misreading of history, White praised five heroes who overcame the blighted ignorance of religion and ushered in modernity: Nicholas Copernicus, Johannes Kepler, Galileo Galilei, Rene Descartes, and Isaac Newton. Unfortunately for his argument, historian Mark Noll points out, "All five of these pioneering" figures "were traditional Christians. . . . None of them believed their scientific work undermined what they considered the main affirmation of the historical Christian faith."[3]

In sum, as historian Ronald Numbers writes, "the greatest myth in the history of science and religion holds that they have been in a state of constant conflict."[4] One common caricature is of a totalitarian church using terror and the threat of violence to try fruitlessly to curb a burgeoning intellectualism in the early modern period. Galileo is often depicted as one of the first martyrs to these developments. His case is significant mostly for what it tells us about how readily exaggerated narratives and false dichotomies take hold in the Western mind. To take the case of Galileo as illustrative of this distorted narrative, the philosopher Paul Feyerabend points out that the judgment to silence Galileo (who was arguing for a sun-centered cosmos) was made by the church "without reference to the faith, or the Church doctrine, but was based exclusively on the scientific situation at the time. It was shared by many outstanding scientists (Tycho Brahe having been one of them)— *and it was correct* when based on the facts, the theories, and the standards of the time."[5] The story "that the church unanimously sided against Galileo and in support of church dogma is simplistic and factually wrong," writes another.[6]

In a similar way, nineteenth-century mythologies portrayed Columbus as defying the ignorance of court clerics by venturing to the New World. Actually, his efforts relied upon the work of Pierre d'Ailly, later a cardinal.[7] In sum, writes one intellectual historian, the term *medieval* should be more accurately associated with "a rounded university education, for careful and critical reading of all kinds of texts, for openness to ideas from all over the world, for a healthy respect for the mysterious and unknown."[8] Another historian agrees: "The word *medieval* is often used as a synonym for muddle-headedness, but it can be more accurately used to indicate . . . meticulous reasoning, that is to say, *clarity*."[9] By the end of that era, one of the best measures of the respect the Christian tradition had for education and intellect, and the reciprocal influence that education and intellect had on Christianity, is this unsurprising fact: the major religious movers and shakers of the Reformation—from John Wyclif to Jan Hus to Martin Luther to John Calvin—were university professors.[10]

That religious institutions and authorities have at times suppressed innovation, stifled inquiry, and punished intellectual dissent is certainly true. However, the ampler narrative of medieval faith and intellect should properly begin with the fact that in the case of the English-speaking people, the introduction of Christianity transformed the intellectual culture—in positive ways. "Not until the acceptance of Christianity by the Saxons," writes a historian, does there come "any abiding interest in letters."[11] "Schools in England," writes another, "are coeval with the coming of Christianity." Rome imported its Christianity to England in the sixth century and, "as a necessary concomitant, schools."[12] Monks compiled chronicles and wrote poetry, kings became conversant in Latin, and copyists preserved ballads and epics and classical literature. An eighth-century library inventory lists works by the great church fathers, but also the philosophical works of Aristotle, treatises of Cicero, the natural history of Pliny, and the poetry of Virgil and Lucan.[13]

In the major study of the printed word in the Middle Ages, George Putnam describes how "after the disappearance of the civilization of the Roman state," the church took over the preservation of culture and literacy that had previously been under the stewardship of the emperors. The church now maintained "throughout the confusion and social disorganization of the early Middle Ages" all "intellectual interests [and] literary activities." Scriptoriums replaced private copyists, and monastic libraries replaced the collections of the Roman elite." Putnam notes that "the incentive to literary labor was no longer the Laurel crown of the circus [or] the favors of a patron, . . . but the glory of God and the service of the church. Upon these agencies depended the existence of literature during the seven long centuries between the fall of the western empire and the beginning of the work of the universities."[14]

In Europe as a whole, most of the schools that developed in the Middle Ages were cathedral schools. As the name implies, they were associated with the great cathedrals, staffed by the clergy or other qualified teachers, and educated priests and laypersons alike. Sometime in the twelfth century, the great cathedral school of Paris was evolving into the first university in the Western world. By the end of the medieval period, more than eighty universities had appeared across the European landscape, each constituting "an association of masters and scholars [students] leading the common life of learning."[15] These schools and universities were not simple seminaries for priests. What set the Paris school apart from all others and the reason it became a model for those to follow was that it "was the first to embrace all the arts and sciences, and therefore first became a university."[16] This is why historians can write that the scientific and intellectual revolutions, when they came, were not a product of classical, but of Christian, culture.[17] (And in America, for the first two full centuries after colonization, every university was founded by a church).[18]

Many "historians have observed that Christian churches were for a crucial millennium leading patrons of natural philosophy and science, in that they supported theorizing experimentation, observation, exploration, documentation, and publication."[19] Even in the field of religion, institutions of higher learning were, as a rule, dedicated to exploration and elaboration rather than dogmatic instruction. The figure who towered above his contemporaries in this early age of higher learning was Pierre Abelard (1079–1142). Though a devout Christian, like virtually all his contemporaries in Europe, he "made questioning and disagreement the royal road to God's truth."[20] David Bentley Hart notes in passing "the long and venerable tradition of Christianity's critical examination and reexamination of its own historical, spiritual, and metaphysical claims."[21]

The great European universities were, then, a Christian innovation. Few scholars of any stripe dispute the plain facts, as the historian Edwin Judge summarizes: "The modern world is the product of a revolution in scientific method. . . . Both experiment in science, and the citing of sources as evidence in history, arise from the worldview of Jerusalem, not Athens, from Jews and Christians, not the Greeks." As C.S. Lewis sums it up, "Men became scientific because they expected Law in Nature, and they expected Law in Nature because they believed in a Legislator."[22]

Consequently, the medieval universities did not just preserve what today we call the liberal arts—they sought to understand the workings of the natural world and pioneered breakthrough technologies. Monks studied—and taught—a whole lot more than Christian dogma. Two intellectual historians note, for instance, that "monasteries not only preserved learning through centuries of civilizational collapse but forged new links from the study of written texts to the marking and measurement of time."[23] And so we find the Abbey of St Albans, dating to the eighth century, in which

> the cloister itself was decorated to reflect the breadth of monastic learning, with Windows depicting leading figures of the liberal arts. The Windows included classical philosophers and poets, of course, but also medical thinkers, mathematicians like Pythagoras and Boethius, and Guido of Arezzo, the monk thought to have designed a hand mnemonic for musical theory. Geometry and astronomy were represented by the totemic Greek Masters Euclid and Ptolemy, and astrology by the ninth century Persian

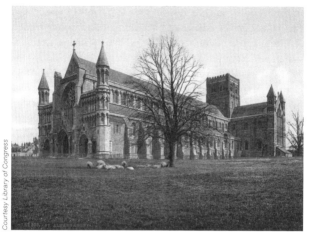

Figure 3. Abbey of St Albans

Albumasar.... Significant recent thinkers in law and theology—Jewish as well as Christian theology—had their own windows, showing that the monks could appreciate both new ideas and the achievements of non-Christians.[24]

St Albans was not an outlier. In 1336, the Pope actually directed that monasteries should send at least one in twenty of their monks for higher education. Female religious figures got into the act as well in the twelfth century. Herrad, abbess of Hohenberg, devised computational tools for her nuns, wrote a compendious guide to the arts, and paid special respect to "Lady Philosophy."[25]

No wonder David Bentley Hart could write with no exaggeration, "Christianity has been the single most creative cultural, ethical, aesthetic, social, political [and] spiritual force in the history of the West."[26] Christianity also laid the foundations of the Western intellectual heritage that was more often seen as a friend than as a foe of religious faith. This heritage was dominant up until the period called—sometimes with too much self-congratulation—the Enlightenment. And yet, even in that watershed era, where rationalism and scientism were to find new dominance, a respect for the powers of reason and their place in the edifice of both human and divine understanding could be found. In that period's principal organ of systematic knowledge in the English-speaking world—the 1771 *Encyclopedia Britannica*—we find it affirmed that "if we cannot comprehend the Supreme Being by our senses, we may discover his attributes by our reason, almost as clearly as we distinguish the properties of matter."[27]

That Latter-day Saints should appreciate the spiritual, as well as the intellectual, achievements of Christianity in the preceding centuries is manifest in the words of the Church's third prophet, John Taylor: "There were [people] in those dark ages who could commune with God. And who, by the power of faith, could draw aside the curtain of eternity and gaze upon the invisible world. There were those who could gaze upon the face of God, have the ministering of angels, and unfold the future destinies of the world. If those were dark ages I pray God to give me a little darkness."[28]

SECTION II
RESTORATION

CHAPTER 3

HEART AND MIND UNITED

Joseph Smith made intelligence an attribute of divinity and a central principle of the Zion ideal. He explicitly linked the gathering and "compact society" to the facilitating of education and envisioned heaven as an eternal continuation of the educative purposes of mortality. He founded a press, a library, a museum, and a university—enacting at great sacrifice his aspirations for a holy and educated people.

Barely a year after the Church's organization, Joseph Smith began the process of building Zion in earnest, naming Jackson County, Missouri, as the place of gathering. Scouting out the area ahead of the first convert immigrants, Joseph was shocked by the rawness of the frontier and its old settlers. "Looking into the vast wilderness of those who sat in darkness," he later noted, "how natural it was to observe the degradation, leanness of intellect, ferocity, and jealousy of a people that were nearly a century behind the times, and to feel for those who roamed about without benefit of civilization, refinement, or religion."[1] Desperate for reassurance that he was not leading his people into a land of hopeless barbarism, he received a revelation that insisted this was indeed "the land which [God] appointed and consecrated for the gathering of the saints, . . . the land of promise and the place for the city of Zion" (Doctrine and Covenants 57:1–2). The focal point of the gathering, the focus of all their material and spiritual efforts, was to be a temple—the first temple to be initiated in this new dispensation, in Jackson County. Joseph wasted no time; two weeks after the command, on August 3, he dedicated a site for the temple.

Little noted in Church history is an event that took place the day before—a gesture of immense symbolic significance for the new faith. On August 2, twelve elders, representing the twelve tribes of Israel, ceremoniously placed the first log for the first building in Zion. It was not for the temple—it was a foundation for a building that would serve as a schoolhouse.[2] Only the next day did Joseph dedicate the temple site. Secular learning, the implicit message held, was a natural and even an essential preparation for spiritual knowledge. In fact, Joseph considered such learning one of the motives of the gathering itself. "One of the principal objects . . . of our coming together," he wrote, "is to obtain the advantages of education; and in order to do this, compact society is absolutely necessary."[3]

Education loomed large in the early Restoration, and it quickly acquired an impressive range and basis in Restoration scripture. The growing canon described revelation itself as a process involving "mind and . . . heart" (Doctrine and Covenants 8:1); "intelligence" was equated with "the glory of God" (Doctrine and Covenants 93:29); salvation—the process of becoming like God, could unfold "no faster than a man gains knowledge";[4] and disciples were instructed that "whatever knowledge or intelligence" we gain in this life has a direct bearing on our positioning to continue that process of learning "in the world to come" (Doctrine and Covenants 130:18–19). Joseph even excerpted in the Church newspaper the views of a contemporary he admired, Thomas Dick. The latter wrote that men and angels in a future state would continue their intellectual progress in mathematics and astronomy as a simple precondition for understanding the glory and majesty of the heavens they inherit. Dick also enumerated natural philosophy, anatomy, physiology, and history as "some of those branches of science which will be recognized [and studied] by the righteous in a future state."[5]

In sum, Joseph preached, "The principle of knowledge is the principle of salvation," and again, "The relationship we have with God places us in a situation to advance in knowledge."[6] Salvation itself, rather than an event or state, was described as an incremental process, one involving the perpetual acquisition of greater understanding. "This is a wide field for the operation of man," said Brigham Young, "that reaches into eternity."[7] "When you climb up a ladder," Joseph explained, "you must begin at the bottom rung. You have got to . . . go on until you have learned the last principle of the Gospel. It will be a great while after the grave before you learn to understand. . . . It is not all to be comprehended in this world."[8] Damnation was anything short of such an eternal journey; for the damned, "there is an end of his career in knowledge, he cannot obtain all knowledge for he has sealed up the gate."[9] Life in this scheme is not so much a trial as an educative experience. Joseph, Brigham, and other Latter-day Saints did not just preach such principles—they acted upon them to found institutions, both official and unofficial, that fostered and nurtured the life of the mind. And as became disconcertingly evident, the Restoration did not buy into what would later become the "two magisterial" doctrine. Learning was learning, whether it involved the periodic table or the ordering of eternal societies.

Back in Ohio months later, Joseph pronounced his 1832 "olive leaf" revelation, in which he announced the inauguration of a "school of the prophets" to be held in a temple built for that (and other) purposes (see Doctrine and Covenants 88). In January 1833, on the second floor of the Newel K. Whitney store, the school commenced operation. In those cold, drafty chambers, fourteen elders and high priests undertook to study "things both in heaven and in the earth, and under the earth; things which have been, things which are, things which must shortly come to pass; things which are at home, things which are abroad; the wars and perplexities of the nations, and the judgments which are on the land; and a knowledge also of the countries and of kingdoms." To this course of study was added the injunction to "become acquainted with all good books, and with languages, tongues, and people" (Doctrine and Covenants 88:79; 90:16). A later revelation adds the command to "obtain a knowledge of history, and of countries, and of kingdoms, of laws of God and man" (Doctrine and Covenants 93:53). So in the Kirtland School of the Prophets, Joseph and other men studied the scriptures and theology—but also German and eventually Hebrew. And not only languages were studied, but also history, geography, mathematics, and topics of current interest. Parley P. Pratt led a Missouri version of the school that summer.

Brigham Young summarized Latter-day Saint views on the value of knowledge: "We are not at all under the necessity of falling into the mistake that the Christian world falls into. They think, when they are handling or dealing in the things of this world, that those things have nothing to do with their religion. Our religion takes within its wide embrace not only things of heaven, but also things of earth. It circumscribes all art, science, and literature pertaining to heaven, earth, and hell."[10] In other words—and here is where we need to recognize a distinctive feature of Restoration teachings—there is no learning that is not, ultimately, tied to our eternal progress now and in the eternities. The utter unity of spiritual and secular truth was most manifest in one of Brigham's most disconcerting—and refreshingly logical—claims: "When the elements melt with fervent heat, the Lord Almighty will send forth his angels, who are well instructed in chemistry, and they will separate the elements and make new combinations thereof."[11] The image of angelic chemists is jarring, but the intellectual adventuresomeness of the point is wonderfully self-consistent. Truth is truth, now and in eternity. No magic wands and no shortcuts; godliness and its powers are

Figure 4. Kirtland School of the Prophets

the consequence of uncompromising intellectual (as well as moral) labor.

Orson Pratt would elaborate this view a few years later: "The study of science is the study of something eternal. If we study astronomy, we study the works of God. If we study chemistry, geology, optics, or any other branch of science, every new truth we come to the understanding of is eternal; it is a part of the great system of universal truth. It is truth that exists throughout universal nature; and God is the dispenser of all truth—scientific, religious, and political."[12]

For Joseph to found a school of the prophets at a time when the Saints were struggling to build the Church in two widely disparate communities and settle and feed hundreds of impoverished immigrants, not to mention his continued labors as a translator and revelator, was nothing short of astounding. The initiative reveals in stark terms the Church's heritage of commitment to the life of the mind, even at great cost. The contemporary relevance of Joseph's school of the prophets, however, might be seen in the timing of his prophetic career: *after* the youthful leader had established his credentials as prophet and translator, *after* he had shown he could use seer stones, the Urim and Thummim, and the unaided powers of revelation to restore truth, he began to slog away at learning languages the old-fashioned way: long hours of study, hitting the books day after day. By study and by faith, intellect added to spiritual gifts—these were principles he enacted.

Later, in late January 1836, what Joseph referred to as the Hebrew School got seriously underway. A Jewish scholar contracted to teach forty students, but the number quickly grew to eighty and beyond, organized into four classes that met six days a week. "Spent the day reading," "spent the day studying German," and "spent the day studying Hebrew" became common entries in Joseph's journal over ensuing weeks. "O may God give me learning, even language; and endue me with qualifications to magnify His name," he prayed.[13]

Even witnesses hostile to the Saints were impressed with the success of Joseph's intellectual agenda. One such observer noted that in spite of the impoverished condition of converts and immigrating New York Saints,

> the Mormons appear to be very eager to acquire education. Men, women and children lately attended school, and they are now employing Mr. Seixas, the Hebrew teacher, to instruct them in Hebrew; and about seventy men in middle life, from twenty to forty years of age, are most eagerly engaged in the study. They pursue their studies alone until twelve o'clock at night, and attend to nothing else. Of course many make rapid progress. I noticed some fine looking and intelligent men among them.... They are by no means, as a class, men of weak minds.[14]

Indeed, Joseph managed to gather to his inner circle a modestly impressive group of men, with a concentration of educational backgrounds unusual in a frontier setting. In addition to his own father, his close associates Oliver Cowdery, Sidney Rigdon, William E. McLellin, and Orson Hyde had all taught school prior to the Church's organization. In fact, of the first eighty converts to the fledgling faith identified by profession, eleven were schoolteachers.[15]

One of the most highly educated first-generation Saints was Wilford Woodruff, who after finishing common school attended an academy for four years, where he studied classical languages along with chemistry, mathematics, and other advanced subjects. Converted to the Church in 1833, he left on a mission a year later. In the midst of preaching throughout the Tennessee Valley he still found time, his journal records, to study Hebrew, English grammar, and a book on philosophy. Returning to Kirtland after his mission, he resumed his study of Greek and Latin in 1836.[16]

Even more advanced in his training was Lorenzo Snow, who joined the Church in that same year. His sister Eliza remembered him as "ever a student, at home as well as in school, (most of his schooling after his twelfth year was during the winter terms,) his book was his constant companion when disengaged from filial duties; and when sought by his associates, 'hid up with his book' became proverbial. With the exception of one term in a High School in Ravenna, Ohio, also a special term of tuition under a Hebrew professor, he completed his scholastic training in Oberlin College."[17]

It wasn't just leaders and missionaries whom Joseph wanted to benefit from education. The Latter-day Saints were unusually progressive on the subject of female education as well. Through both informal and formal channels, women found access to educational opportunities. Sarah Kimball, for example—who would go on to become a foremost intellectual, suffrage crusader, and women's leader—attended the school of the prophets alongside the men while still a teenager. Although women didn't participate in the Hebrew School, in some cases they benefited at one remove. Caroline Crosby, for instance, was instructed daily by her husband upon his return from the Hebrew School—and she eventually acquired reading proficiency. Girls were admitted to the Kirtland High School, even though Eliza R. Snow ran her own "select school" for young women as well. A few years later, a Judge Thorp of Clay County, Missouri, witness to the Saints' migration into

Illinois, observed that Latter-day Saint women were "generally well educated and as a rule were quite intelligent."[18] In 1842, the issue of female education was explicitly broached when a Nauvoo Lyceum was held on the question "Should Females be educated to the same extent of Males?" The verdict they came to is not known, but county records show that over half the students enrolled in Nauvoo's schools were female. It has even been suggested that the Saints' liberal views on the equality of the sexes were in part responsible for the hostility to the Church in Illinois. Those high schools accepting girls in this decade were still not the rule; in Cleveland, Ohio, for instance, girls were admitted in 1847, but "against the protest of the principal."[19]

With the removal of the Church to Nauvoo in 1839, the Saints' educational agenda became even more ambitious. When Latter-day Saints settled there, only one in six children in the upper Mississippi Valley had access to public education; in Illinois, as few as one in fourteen actually attended school.[20] Eliza R. Snow initiated a three-month curriculum for women in a room over Nauvoo's Masonic Lodge.[21] Joseph and Adelia Cole advertised tuition rates for twelve-week quarters in their Nauvoo Seminary, held in a room above Joseph Smith's store. Reading, writing, and spelling were a packaged bargain at two dollars, but the course in astronomy cost twice that. Harold and Martha Coray were so successful with their school that they rented the 150-seat capacity music hall and nearly filled it.[22]

In 1841, Joseph described an ambitious new project—the University of Nauvoo. This university, he wrote, "will enable us to teach our children wisdom, to instruct them in all the knowledge and learning, in the arts, science and learned professions. We hope to make this institution one of the great lights of the world."[23] Several men served as professors, including Sidney Rigdon and Orson Spencer, himself a college and seminary graduate. Orson Pratt, an astronomer as well as a mathematician, was the most accomplished and soon emerged as the primary force behind the university. William W. Phelps called Pratt the "gauge of philosophy," and he probably had no intellectual equal in the Church's first century.

The ambitious curriculum of the University of Nauvoo included courses in chemistry and geology and several areas of mathematics, literature, philosophy, history, religion, music, and foreign languages (German, French, Latin, Greek, and Hebrew). To supplement the university, the Saints started an impressive library and had plans for a museum as well. A newspaper reported that

> among the improvements going forward in this city, none merit higher praise, than the Seventies' Library. The concern has been commenced on a footing and scale, broad enough to embrace the arts and sciences, every where: so that the Seventies' while traveling over the face of the globe, as the Lord's "Regular Soldiers," can gather all the curious things, both natural and artificial, with all the knowledge, inventions, and wonderful specimens of genius that have been gracing the world for almost six thousand years. Ten years ago but one seventy, and now "fourteen seventies" and the foundation for the best library in the world! It looks like old times when they had "Kirjath Sapher [sic]," the city of books.[24]

As for books in the lives of Nauvoo residents, minutes of the Nauvoo Library and Literary Institute suggest that the members' tastes in reading at this time tended more to the intellectual than the frivolous; patrons shunned novels but inclined toward history and philosophy. John Locke's *Essay Concerning Human Understanding*; biographies of Napoleon; and English, French, and American histories circulated frequently. Among the books Joseph donated to the library were Thomas Dick's *Philosophy of a Future State*, Mosheim's *Church History*, and the *Histoire de Charles*.[25]

A few years later, on December 23, 1847, Brigham Young, at "Winter Quarters, Omaha Nation, west bank of Missouri River, near Council Bluffs, North America," performed one of his last tasks as President of the Quorum of the Twelve

LET'S TALK ABOUT FAITH AND INTELLECT

Apostles (he would be sustained as Joseph's successor and President of the Church four days later). As he directed members in the best routes by which to assemble in the West, giving counsel for preparations and the execution of the arduous trek, he included this exhortation, as "made manifest by [God's] Spirit":

> It is very desirable that all the Saints should improve every opportunity of securing at least a copy of every valuable treatise on education—every book, map, chart, or diagram that may contain interesting, useful, and attractive matter, to gain the attention of children, and cause them to love to learn to read; and, also every historical, mathematical, philosophical, geographical, geological, astronomical scientific, practical, and all other variety of useful and interesting writings, maps, &c., to present to the General Church Recorder, when they shall arrive at their destination, from which important and interesting matter may be gleaned to compile the most valuable works, on every science and subject, for the benefit of the rising generation.
>
> We have a printing press, and any who can take good printing or writing paper to the valley will be blessing themselves and the Church. We also want all kinds of mathematical and philosophical instruments, together with all rare specimens of natural curiosities and works of art that can be gathered and brought to the valley, where, and from which, the rising generation can receive instruction; and if the Saints will be diligent in these matters, we will soon have the best, the most useful and attractive museum on the earth.[26]

The intellectual culture of a people, like the commitment of an individual, is measured by what they do when they are not required by law or by their church to pursue studies. In the case of the Utah Latter-day Saints, a number of independent initiatives revealed great interest at the popular level in the life of the mind. In 1854, the Saints had been in the Salt Lake Valley less than seven years. That winter, at Lorenzo Snow's large and spacious house, several men and women met to participate in the newly organized Polysophical Society. They played instruments (from the piano to the bagpipes), sang, recited original poetry, and discoursed extemporaneously. The small group swelled with members anxious to enrich their minds and souls with a healthy dose of refinement in the midst of a cultural and agricultural desert. Outgrowing the private home of Snow, the society soon occupied the public Seventies Hall and occasionally the capacious Social Hall.

In February 1855, sixty men met in the Salt Lake City Council House and formed the Universal Scientific Society, with Wilford Woodruff as president. Woodruff expressed the society's goals in a presidential address: "We are desirous of learning and possessing every truth which will exact and benefit mankind. . . . We wish to be made acquainted . . . with art, science, or any other subject which has ever proved of benefit to God, angels or men." The society went on to establish their own library, reading room, and museum.[27]

In this same decade, B. H. Roberts belonged to the Young Men's Club of Centerville, Utah. This remarkable, independent group of boys paid the then-hefty initiation fee of $2.50 (and $0.50 monthly), "all of which was turned into books." The group existed expressly "to encourage reading and meet . . . at stated period—usually once a week—and to retell the stories of their reading." They amassed "a rather considerable library" and even raised enough funds to build their own public hall.[28]

Beginning in 1869, Orson Pratt conducted observations from an adobe observatory that he had built in the shadow of the rising Salt Lake Temple. The image of the temple and the observatory is an image that hovers in the background of Latter-day Saint culture, affirming one of the tradition's most beautiful paradoxes: that the certainties revealed in the Church's temples never overwhelm the passionate love of learning that fired the mind and spirit of the tradition's founders.

As in Nauvoo, Utah Saints were unusually progressive in

LET'S TALK ABOUT FAITH AND INTELLECT

Figure 5. Orson Pratt Observatory

the area of female education. When the University of Deseret reopened in 1868 after a hiatus of some years, women composed almost 50 percent of the class. (At this time, women in America received less than fifteen percent of bachelor's degrees awarded; all told, only 0.7 percent of American women eighteen to twenty-one years of age were attending college in 1870.)[29]

Brigham Young said, "We believe that women . . . should . . . study law or physics or become good bookkeepers and be able to do the business in any counting house." He also advised women to attend medical schools; consequently, the women's Relief Society supported a number of sisters who went east to obtain training. Romania B. Pratt Penrose, Ellis Shipp, and Margaret Shipp Roberts (sister wives), together with Martha Hughes Cannon and many others, returned with degrees in hand to establish practices and teach classes. Eliza Snow even attempted to establish a Female Medical College so Utah could train its own women doctors.[30] By the turn of the century, more female American medical students hailed from Utah than from any other state in the union.[31]

HEART AND MIND UNITED

In 1870, Utah children attended school at a higher rate than in New York, Pennsylvania, or Massachusetts, the birthplace of public education. Even so, Brigham Young in that year ratcheted up the level of institutional support by establishing a series of academies (tuition-supported high schools) throughout the settlements. Three years after Young's death, there were some two dozen of these academies from Canada to Mexico. In 1880, according to the census, Utah's literacy rate (for ages ten and above) was 95 percent, whereas in the country as a whole, it was 87 percent.[32]

In Provo, Brigham Young Academy was organized in 1875. A century later, President Spencer W. Kimball described the synthesis of faith and intellect that its successor institution, Brigham Young University, aspires to embody: "The faculty has a double heritage that they must pass along: the secular knowledge that history has washed to the feet of mankind along with the new knowledge brought by scholarly research, and also the vital and revealed truths that have been sent to us from heaven."[33]

In a remarkable sermon he delivered on the nature of man and human happiness, Brigham Young made the unceasing pursuit of knowledge not just an ingredient in salvation, but the essence of the only joy humankind will find fulfilling:

> All men should study to learn the nature of mankind, and to discern that divinity inherent in them. A spirit and power of research is planted within, yet they remain undeveloped. . . . What will satisfy us? If we understood all principles and powers that are, that have been, and that are to come, and had wisdom sufficient to control powers and elements with which we are associated, perhaps we would then be satisfied. If this will not satisfy the human mind, there is nothing that will. . . . If we could so understand true philosophy as to understand our own creation, and what it is for . . . and could understand that matter can be organized and brought forth into intelligence, and to possess more intelligence, and to continue to increase in that intelligence; and could learn those principles that

Figure 6. Brigham Young Academy, ca. 1900

organized matter into animals, vegetables, and into intelligent beings; and could discern the Divinity acting, operating, and diffusing principles into matter to produce intelligent beings, and to exalt them—to what? Happiness. Will nothing short of that fully satisfy the spirits implanted within us? No.[34]

The first fifty years of the Restoration, we can see, established an impressive record for living up to the ideal of learning by study and by faith (see Doctrine and Covenants 109:7). In those same years and into the first decades of the twentieth century, several intellectual developments rocked the Christian world—especially the birth of biblical archaeology, evolutionary science, and higher criticism (an approach to scripture that filtered the Bible through the prism of secular scholarship). Faith and intellect were finding an uneasy alliance, as Catholics and Protestants alike struggled with "the crisis of Modernism," a movement to reinterpret church teachings in the light of nineteenth-century developments of a more historical consciousness.

Latter-day Saints of today's era have been experiencing their own reappraisal of our past. Greater access to the archives, more rigorous historical methods, and pressures for more transparency have all contributed to new questions and challenges for the faithful. To these shifts, the leadership of the Church has responded by endorsing and encouraging rigorous intellectual engagement with the faith. Elder M. Russell Ballard signaled this spirit of inquiry when he told Church educators, "As Church education moves forward in the 21st century, each of you needs to consider any changes you should make in the way you prepare to teach, how you teach, and what you teach. . . . Mostly, our young people lived a sheltered life. Our curriculum at that time, though well-meaning, did not prepare students for today—a day when students have instant access to virtually everything about the Church from every possible point of view."

Elder Ballard continued, "Gone are the days when a student asked an honest question and a teacher responded, 'Don't worry about it!' Gone are the days when a student raised a sincere concern and a teacher bore his or her testimony as a response intended to avoid the issue." Then, directly countering the anti-intellectual attacks and controversy avoidance of the 1980s, he recast honest scholars as assets rather than challengers of the faith. "If necessary, we should ask those with appropriate academic training, experience, and expertise for help." "If you have questions" about historical issues, he continued, "ask someone who has studied them."[35] Elder Neil L. Andersen affirmed this approach: "Addressing honest questions is an important part of building faith, and we use both our intellect and our feelings."[36] President Russell M. Nelson summed up the case concisely: we should have a "sacred regard for intellect."[37]

CHAPTER 4

THE PROBLEM OF GOD, GOOD, AND EVIL

Joseph Smith's question "Which church is true?" is a starting point for religious conversation far beyond where many in the world—and some in the Church—find themselves. Is belief in the supernatural itself even reasonable? Does the Restoration convincingly address the problem of evil?

In Auschwitz, a thirsty prisoner reached out the window of his bleak hut for an icicle. A guard, spotting the action, knocked it from his hand before he could find even that scant relief. "Why?" asked Primo Levi. "Here there is no why," replied the brutal guard. Having both seen and experienced the worst that one human can do to another, Levi later wrote, "If there is an Auschwitz, then there cannot be a God." Decades later, he added in pencil, "I find no solution to the riddle. I see, but I do not find it." Then, devoid of a solution to life's most terrible question, he took his own life.[1]

In the face of unimaginable human suffering, and in the presence of unspeakable evil in the world, it is important to say this at the outset: even the gospel does not have an answer to every question, an explanation for every experience through which we pass. Religious faith and intellectual aspiration alike operate best in a climate of humility, where amid the search for understanding we recognize the limitations of our vision. However, the Restoration *does* provide a satisfactory theological framework in which we can begin to make sense of the coexistence of a benevolent God and the moral atrocities and natural calamities that surround us. In part, this is because Restoration conceptions of God avoid the insuperable problems that are implicit in conventional doctrines of the Divine and that have been pointed out for centuries.

The classic problem of evil is simply expressed: evil exists; either God is *unable* to prevent it (in which case He is not omnipotent, perfectly powerful), or He is *unwilling* to prevent it (in which case He is not omnibenevolent, perfectly good). Given this stark choice, most influential thinkers in the Christian tradition opted to preserve omnipotence, at the cost of what most would understand as perfect goodness. Hence, in this view of absolute sovereignty, God "at his own pleasure arranged the fall of the first man and in him the ruin of his posterity,"[2] for "nothing takes place but as [God] wills it."[3]

Even assuming that God chooses to respect our freedom to hurt and abuse and kill one another, if He is the Creator of all that exists, including our souls, why did He not endow us with more beautiful, kindly souls? A twentieth-century philosopher pointed out this most obvious, fatal flaw in the orthodox view of God: If He created our souls, He "could have prevented all sin by creating us with better natures and in more favorable surroundings."[4] He chose not to. We find ourselves to be inclined by nature toward selfishness and sin. So in this view He is God the omnipotent, the all-powerful Creator. But He is not omnibenevolent because He did not create our souls in a way that predispositioned us all for salvation.

Restoration thought embraces the other horn of the dilemma. Joseph Smith restored a God of infinite goodness and kindness but not infinite creative power, with words unique in the Christian tradition. "God himself is a self-existent god.... Who told you that man did not exist in like manner upon the same principle?... Intelligence is eternal and exists upon a self-existent principle. It is a spirit from age to age and there is no creation about it.... [We are] self-existent with God."[5] So the core of our being, spirit, or "intelligence," is not something that God made. The scope of our innate potential for good and evil is tied, in essential ways, to our nature; and that nature is constituted, at its most fundamental level, by an identity that God did not create or impose on us. When that nature, shaped but not determined by contingent factors like environment and genetics, is freed to act out its own inclinations and desires, the consequences range from the goodness of Anne Frank to the evils of Auschwitz. The freedom to enact the good requires the freedom to perpetrate evil. Meaningful freedom cannot exist without the freedom to act in both ways. This is why, as C. S. Lewis put it with economical and irrefutable logic, "either something or nothing must depend on individual choices. And if something, who could set bounds to it?"[6] Our capacity to inflict hurt and suffering upon each other is virtually unlimited and is not attributable to God. "Hence," writes Nicolai Berdyaev, "our attitude to evil must be twofold: we must be tolerant of it as the Creator is tolerant, and we must mercilessly struggle against it. There is no escaping from this paradox, as it is rooted in freedom and the very fact of a distinction between good and evil."[7]

This conclusion leaves us with the other half of the good-and-evil problem unresolved—suffering that is not the fruit of moral agency. The child of a colleague of mine suffered from an ALS-type syndrome. His father and his mother bore the incomprehensible pain of watching their little beloved son, step by horrific step, atrophy piecemeal. He slowly lost all physical and then mental functioning, until death released him. Tsunamis, cancers, and death by a thousand other natural causes are not (generally) the consequence of willful human choices. No personal agency is being safeguarded in these cases. Could a compassionate God have not protected us against those forms of suffering that are outside of human control? Can we in good conscience maintain that watching a pure little child waste away from a horrific disease is necessary for our spiritual growth? It is here, once again, where humility must intrude and demand that we not try to resolve the problem with facile comforts. The suffering of another is sacred terrain; we risk desecrating it when we presume to neatly salve their spiritual anguish with our frail verbal medicines.

A Latter-day Saint can, however, suggest that, as a general rule, it is with our souls as it is with those laws that govern our physical world. "The elements are eternal," Restoration scripture holds (Doctrine and Covenants 93:33). And God is He who most perfectly understands and operates in harmony with the laws that govern those eternal elements. For a Latter-day Saint, whether in the realm of moral law or physical law, they are eternal and immutable. As Parley P. Pratt explained, "These are principles of eternal truth, they are laws which cannot be broken, . . . whether the reckoning be calculated by the Almighty, or by man."[8] One ancient prophet even intimates that God's position as God actually depends on His respect for and observance of these eternal laws (else God "would cease to be God" [Alma 42:13]). To enter into the world of natural law is to be subject to the tragic nature of that world: its bleak indifference to human valuations, its blindness to human suffering.

But God is not indifferent, and unless we are clockwork deists who deny God the power to intervene in human affairs, then we believe God can and does intercede at times to rescue, to save, to succor. In that case, how do we account for the unevenness of God's response to human suffering? Why indifference at my doorstep and a miracle next door? We cannot know. The calculus is too complex when one tries to factor in the varying efficacy of faith-laden prayers, the infinitely branching consequences of a divine interposition, the sanctifying potential of human pain, and our resilient tendency to revert to a baseline of temperament in the aftermath of miraculous manifestations and catastrophic disappointments alike.

From another angle, we can see how our limited perspective may misread the problem of human exposure to evil. We cannot know what sufferings we *have* been spared, what interventions, personal and global *have* transpired in our lives or in history. At the same time, there seems also to be a Boyle's law of suffering at work in the human psyche. A gas will expand to fill any space that is available to it. So does the elimination of one pain (recovery from a serious illness, for example) create a space, which is immediately filled by our absorption in the next pain that rushes in to fill the vacuum (the chronic pain remaining). A moment's reflection will suggest that on a scale of infinite possibilities for pain, no matter how much suffering we have been spared, no matter what bounds the laws of God or of nature and human biology have set, the question would remain the same: cannot God alleviate *this* suffering? Only in a world of imperturbable sameness, uniformity, and emotional insulation from all disequilibrium would this question never arise.

Some skeptics—Christian and nonbelievers alike—dismiss any theology of a limited God, incapable of finding a less-anguishing synthesis of growth, freedom, and suffering. They may find such divine limitations either blasphemous or unworthy of regard. Such a God, however, can be infinitely compassionate, have our best interests at heart, and still preside over a realm of pain and suffering, with no contradiction. Such a God would exist as the most intelligent, loving, and powerful being in the universe—without being the source of that universe. To envision such a God, like the weeping God of the Restoration, is to recognize in God a figure who clearly cannot eliminate our tears, subject as He—and we—are to the constraints of the agency of others, the laws of nature, and the necessity of an educative mortality than can reshape us more in His likeness. To the objection that this view of deity risks the possibility of a fallible God who is incapable of fulfilling His promises, David L. Paulsen, one of our tradition's premier philosophers, responds that he trusts God "because He's told us that we can. My faith in God is grounded in His self-disclosures, not in logical inferences from philosophically constructed premises."[9]

Such a God, it seems to me, is infinitely preferable, more worthy of worship and adoration, and more appealing to our instincts for goodness and reasonableness than the God who, in the language of the Christian creeds, is all-powerful, "the source of all that is," and who ordains all that transpires in history and in every individual's life. Ironically, we find ourselves in harmony with atheist Richard Dawkins, who finds a Judeo-Christian God operating outside all bounds of logical or scientific law absurd, because "any creative intelligence of sufficient complexity to design anything comes into existence only at the end product of an extended process of gradual evolution."[10] Elaborating this point, he said that "you have to have a gradual slow incremental process [to explain an eye or a brain] and by the very same token, God would have to have the same kind of explanation. . . . God indeed can't have just happened. If there are gods in the universe, they must be the end product of slow incremental processes. If there are beings in the universe that we would treat as gods, . . . that we would worship . . . as gods, then they must have come about by an incremental process, gradually."[11]

Latter-day Saints believe in a deity who worked in harmony with invariant laws to shape and organize matter. God is an intelligent being, more intelligent than all coexisting intelligences, who went from glory to glory, from "one degree to another from grace to grace, . . . from exaltation to exaltation."[12] The Apostle John Widtsoe elaborated: "By the persistent efforts of will, His recognition of universal laws became greater until he attained at last a conquest over the universe, which to our finite understanding seems absolutely complete. We may be certain that, through self-effort, the inherent and innate powers of God have been developed to a God-like degree. Thus He has become God."[13] An official Church position affirmed that fact in 1909, declaring God "an exalted man, perfected, enthroned, and supreme."[14]

LET'S TALK ABOUT FAITH AND INTELLECT

At the same time, the Church—with teachings unique in the Christian world—has declared that heaven is not a patriarchal monopoly. In 1895, the feminist Elizabeth Cady Stanton pointed to two deficits in the Christian tradition that doomed women to an inferior status: the subordinate role of Eve and a God entirely and solely male.[15] Restoration teachings, with remarkable prescience and inspired equity, redressed both impoverished teachings. Restoration scriptures attribute to Eve a crucial role in the plan of human embodiment; she did not doom her posterity but courageously opened the door of mortality to all (Moses 5:11); as for divine parenthood, the leadership has repeatedly affirmed the truth that "all men and women are in the similitude of the universal Father *and* Mother."[16]

Finally, God *does* inhabit the same universe that we do. He is not a being remote from or existing outside of space and time, transcendent and beyond human categories altogether. He is *in space* as well as *in time*. Philosopher Nicholas Wolterstorff, writing against the grain of centuries of Christian theology, states the seemingly obvious: "Given that all human actions are temporal," he reasons, "those actions of God which are 'response' are temporal as well."[17] That fact is a core motif of the Restoration. Instead of a single unparalleled eruption of the divine into the human in the unique incarnation of Christ, we find a proliferation of historical iterations, which collectively become the ongoing substance rather than the shadow of God's past dealings in the universe.

CHAPTER 5

THE STORIES WE TELL

We cannot survive apart from narratives that give our lives meaning and purpose. The decline of religion in Western Christianity was accompanied by new stories that replaced the old ones. How does the story the Restoration tells compare in rational appeal with the alternatives?

About many things we can profess little to no certainty. We don't even know and cannot prove that other persons are self-aware, having a thinking, feeling, actual self behind the body we see. Yet we are pretty sure those people are real, conscious beings.[1] As one writer on neuroscience notes, this assumption is based on "deeply ingrained intuition" with no "real foundation" behind it.[2] We don't deduce that fact, since it is not logically provable from any known premise. And we don't infer that fact, since we don't have any prior facts that there are other sentient selves we can extrapolate from. So we know with reasonable confidence some things by neither deduction nor induction. We get to that belief about other conscious minds from *abduction*, a perfectly rational process by which we conceive of the best explanation to make sense of the facts we *can* observe. I have an interior, self-conscious mind (or soul). And other people look and behave and seem to experience pain and pleasure like I do. So they probably are not mindless, soulless automatons. They probably have an inner life comparable to mine.

Many—if not most—of our rational operations in life are

of this sort. How did you catch chickenpox? What's causing global warming? Why are you late and your car looks banged up? One looks at a phenomenon or state of affairs and postulates an explanation of how that circumstance came to be, one that sounds reasonable and that comports with our observations. If we hold on to such an explanation in the absence of any corrobative evidence or in the face of incompatible evidence, then our rationality evaporates, and we are in the realm of myth or delusion. If we refuse to make reasonable inferences without proof positive, on the other hand, we will be surprised every time a new sunrise occurs and unprepared every time a traffic light turns red.

Religious faith, in this context, is not "belief without evidence" or "belief against the evidence." It is belief or trust or loyalty consistent with, but not fully substantiated by, all the conceivable evidence. It may begin as an effective hypothesis of the form "Does this particular set of religious claims give a plausible account of who I am, of the yearnings and motivations that guide me at the deepest levels, and of why there is pain and suffering, deplorable evil, but also love and virtue and nobleness of character among my fellow humans? Does that set of claims comport with experience, with reason, and with that same interior compass by which I discern what is good and beautiful?"

Latter-day prophets and scripture give a very definite account of our origin, our place in the universe, and the meaning and purpose of life. We are, they teach, eternal beings, coeternal with God, embarked on one phase in a never-ending pursuit of greater truth and love and light. In Elder Jeffrey Holland's words, "Restored truth taught that God's glory is his intelligence and that it is to be our glory as well."[3] Secular voices believe that though we may have the capacity to create ad hoc meaning or our own personal objectives, as a species we find ourselves here on planet Earth without a divine designer or intended purpose. Creedal Christianity has framed narratives of its own to make sense of life, some of which have been particularly problematic: a God without body, parts, or most troublingly, without passions;[4] a human created for the glory of God and made expressly to serve and honor Him;[5] an original sin, which transmitted both guilt and depravity to Eve and Adam's posterity; and human destinies to which we may be assigned even before creation and independently of either the timing of our birth or quality of our lives. Voices of the Restoration tell a very different story—one consistent with our intuitions of the good and just, but more than just morally satisfying. The Restoration weaves a narrative that is intellectually appealing in its premises, is exhilarating in its possibilities, and turns out to be remarkably consistent with many cutting-edge ideas of leading philosophers and scientists.

"Things Change"

Nobel prize–winning physicist Frank Wilczek writes that all the fundamental laws of the universe "describe how things change."[6] This is a riveting proposition. The quest to understand the cosmos is not about structures and configurations and assemblages, because none of those are fixed or static. The universe, and everything in it, revolves and orbits and combusts and radiates and decays and transforms. And the key to understanding the universe is to apprehend the *way* in which every one of these changes takes place. Metamorphosis pervades cosmic structures, the subatomic realm, and the human mind. That was not always the story men and women of learning had been telling.

In 1789, as revolutionaries in France were reshaping the political order, the leading astronomer of the age, William Herschel, was shifting the cosmic paradigm. His paper on "The Construction of the Heavens," published by the Royal Society in 1785, effected a change in the Western world's cosmic vision more dramatic that Copernicus's replacement of an Earth-centered system by a heliocentric one. For generations of thinkers, God's supreme perfection seemed to suggest that the universe He created was likewise flawless and complete when He laid down His celestial instruments. When He pronounced His labors good and rested from His efforts, the perfectly ordered cosmos had naught to do but hum along in sublime harmony until the end of time.

At first, Herschel's astronomical observations through his telescopes of unprecedented power and precision only confirmed the infinitude of God's domain, revealing star systems beyond star systems in unending procession. But Herschel quickly perceived that he was observing a universe in a process of continual disruption, upheaval, and transformation on a colossal scale. He described "extensive combinations," stars in process of "condensation," others in retreat or in collision. "When, at the same time that a cluster of stars is forming in one part of space, there may be another collecting in a different, but perhaps no far distant quarter, which may occasion a mutual approach towards their common center of gravity. . . . As a natural consequence of the former cases, there will be formed great cavities or vacancies by the retreat of the stars towards the various centers which attract them." The whole was a scene of such violent contestation that he admitted surprise that the entirety did not "tend to a general destruction, by the shock of one star's falling upon another."[7]

Indeed, as one writer has summarized the import of Herschel's shocking discovery, he "completely overturned any residual idea of a stable, overarching, temple-like universe, created once and for all by the great Celestial Architect" and replaced it with a dynamic cosmos of waxing and waning worlds, "fluid movements and changes."[8] Even so, it would be another few centuries before Western civilization's vision of the dynamic, ongoing creation of the cosmos reached its apogee. Writes one historian of science, "When a prominent Belgian scientist proposed in 1927 that the universe was growing in size like an expanding balloon, Einstein pronounced the idea 'abominable.'" Shortly thereafter, Einstein bowed before the irrefutable evidence: "According to current data, our universe will keep expanding forever."[9]

In light of these developments and others, how astonishing

are the words that launch the cosmic epic in Latter-day scripture: "Worlds without number have I created. . . . And as one earth shall pass away, and the heavens thereof even so shall another come; and there is no end to my works" (Moses 1:33, 38). Not only is God the architect of an ongoing Creation, but we as coeternal beings are situated in Restoration teachings within that cosmic story, coparticipating willingly and guidedly in the larger sweep of natural laws of change and development by which we, too, are governed. Joseph taught:

> Intelligence is eternal and exists upon a self-existent principle. It is a spirit from age to age and there is no creation about it. The first principles of man are self-existent with God. All the minds and spirits that God ever sent into the world are susceptible of enlargement and improvement. The relationship we have with God places us in a situation to advance in knowledge. God Himself found Himself in the midst of spirits and glory. Because He was greater He saw proper to institute laws whereby the rest, who were less in intelligence, could have a privilege to advance like Himself and be exalted with Him.[10]

This is a story with no precedent in religious thought: coeternal with God; invited to enter into relationship with Him before the world's creation; a relationship of parent to child, or master to disciple, not king to subject. Change the beginning of the story, and you change everything. All of life's tragedies and epiphanies, bumbling errors and steps forward, pains of the bitter and delights of the sweet, are part of a long-prepared curriculum in gradual sanctification. Like a violin maestro who aspires to mentor his student to a comparable status, God shepherds us through instruction, development, growth, and education, with the goal of making us like Him- (and Her-)self—playing music as beautifully as They, in imitation of the gift and beauty, but not echoing the same score. We are to be neither subjects nor clones, but peers and joint-heirs (see Romans 8). Brigham Young summarized this conception of eternal souls evolving through endless aeons under the guidance of divine beings: "Our divine spirit," he said, would be joined to a body. Then this human soul—body and spirit—work jointly at sanctification "until the body also becomes divine; and then, when all has become divine, we may love all with a divine affection."[11]

Change. Purposeful, ongoing, developmental change is a fundamental of cosmic history, of biological life on earth—and of our eternal existence as human souls. Such change and growth are at the heart of God's creative activity and of each individual human story. How rational and reasonable one's faith in that background story turns out to be. Nothing in the universe is static, and we are part of that dynamism. What distinguishes us from quarks and asteroids and lichen is that we can choose to be taught, to align ourselves with the teachings of a superior Intelligence, and to optimize all of the forces acting upon us from within and without to grow in the way we *choose* to grow. We can aspire to goodness, wisdom, holiness, and change in *those* directions. This is a proposition seconded by personal experience and by some of the best and most creative thinking of our era.

We sense this capacity for independent action, and we suffer distress when it is thwarted—by totalitarian regimes, by uninspired supervisors at work, by physical limitations, or by our own lethargy, bad habits, and addictions. More than an emotional response to interference with our will is at stake in such cases. Freedom to believe, to choose to act—this agency is the essence of our core identity as human souls and is rooted from eternity to eternity as foundational self-determination. The instinctual need to thrive as independently acting agents is—scripture tells us—commensurate with our very being and purposeful presence in the universe. "All truth is independent in that sphere in which God has placed it, to act for itself, *as all intelligence also; otherwise there is no existence*" (Doctrine and Covenants 93:30; emphasis added). This is an inversion of titanic proportions. Intelligence—personal identity in the sense of an eternally existent, independently acting self—is in some sense foundational to rather than a side effect of meaningful existence.

That the human mind—consciousness, or "intelligence" in Joseph's language—is not just eternal but also foundational to all existence finds resonance among some cutting-edge philosophers and theorists of human consciousness. As cognitive psychologist Donald Hoffman notes, "All attempts at a physicalist theory of consciousness have failed. They have produced no scientific theory and no plausible idea of how to build one."[12] Many philosophers and theorists alike are coming to recognize that no account of what goes on in the brain can in any way explain—or reproduce—the *experience* of consciousness, the *taste* of a lemon, the *sensation* of a fragrant rose, or the *delighted wonder* of our own being. Religious skeptic Steven Pinker concedes that the fact "that it subjectively *feels like something* to be such [brain] circuitry . . . may have to be stipulated as a fact about reality where explanation stops."[13]

The philosopher Thomas Nagel (himself no believer) argues that both rationality and consciousness itself "cannot be conceived of, even speculatively, as composed of countless atoms of miniature rationality. The metaphor of the mind as a computer built out of a huge number of transistor-like homunculi will not serve the purpose. . . . It could account for behavioral output, but not for understanding."[14] To reduce consciousness to a "sheer illusion," fabricated by firing synapses, just atoms in motion (as does the prominent academic Daniel Dennett), is striking more and more theorists of consciousness as patently absurd. This physical reductionism, "the most striking feature of . . . mainstream philosophy of mind in the past fifty years . . . seems obviously false," writes the influential John Searle. Philosopher Galen Strawson agrees: rejecting our common-sense intuitions about the nonmaterial reality of consciousness and conscious states of experiences is "one of the most amazing manifestations of human irrationality on record."[15] And as philosopher David Chalmers wrote in

1994: "No explanation given in wholly physical terms can ever account for the emergence of conscious experience."[16]

And so, concludes Hoffman, in words that echo powerfully Joseph's revelation, "If we grant that there are conscious experiences, and that there are conscious agents that enjoy and act on experiences, then we can try to construct a scientific theory of consciousness that posits that conscious agents—not objects in spacetime—are fundamental."[17] Nobel prize–winning physiologist George Wald writes that "mind, rather than emerging as a late outgrowth in the evolution of life, has always existed as the matrix, the source and condition of physical reality."[18] In other words, now, in the early twenty-first century, some leading intellectuals are positing that existence itself may be traceable to a principle of consciousness that sounds very much like Joseph's "intelligence," which he also described as foundational to existence itself.

These provocative theories about the primacy and irreducibility of consciousness are unfolding even as other kinds of scholars and writers revisit the question of what makes us human and whether we differ from our biological cousins in purely incidental ways. That question lies beyond the domain of empirical proof, but one may find powerful reasons for believing that something more substantive than a very slight variation in DNA sets us apart.[19] (It may be the case, however, that just such a "slight variation" in our DNA orients us toward a uniquely powerful and purposeful capacity for self-transcendence. We may be tempted to forget that because our bodies are in God's image, many of our inclinations that are divinely oriented may be at least in part bodily rooted.)

Consider the example of the child: an infant two months old. When presented with two different patterns, one familiar and one novel, she will show a marked preference for the latter.[20] Before she even knows how to frame a question—or what a question even is—her stance toward life is interrogatory. Children crave the novel, the different, the unexplored, and the unexperienced. It is debatable to what extent language is a uniquely human capacity, since apes, like the accomplished chimpanzee Kanzi, have mastered limited but impressive vocabularies. Yet, as Ian Leslie notes, "What Kanzi never did, and never does, is ask *why*. He never furrows his brow, leans over the keyboard, and bashes out a sentence like, 'Why are you asking me all these questions?' or 'What *exactly* are you trying to discover?' He doesn't ask what lies beyond the confines of his home at the research center."[21] Only humans have what Leslie calls "the fourth drive" (after food, shelter, and reproduction). Only humans are impelled by the desire to expand their world experientially, intellectually.

In gymnastics as in composing a sonata, a Simone Biles as much as a Beethoven is catalyzed by the recognition of an inherent freedom, potential, and capacity to be more than she at present is, to register an impact on the world, to bring into being an excellence that was not there before. This was precisely the point made by Elder Dieter Uchtdorf: "The bounds of creativity extend far beyond the limits of a canvas or a sheet of paper and do not require a brush, a pen, or the keys of a piano. Creation means bringing into existence something that did not exist before: colorful gardens, harmonious homes, family memories, flowing laughter."[22] The Russian philosopher Nikolai Berdyaev, who considers creativity to be our most distinctive human attribute, writes that creativity is always "an ascent"; it is a demonstration of a particular kind of freedom, a "liberation *for the sake of* something." And "every creative act which we perform in relation to other people—an act of love, or pity, of help, of peacemaking—not only has a future but is eternal."[23] These potentialities, and these unrealized relations, are what we are made for, and in their achievement our freedom is most meaningfully manifest and felt.

In designing a microprocessor, as in studying the effect of microloans in Papua New Guinea, one is fulfilling an imperative to change oneself—or the universe—by transmuting the raw materials of the world into order and meaning and substance. Even in the act of learning, one is transforming the world—literally one's mind. "To learn something," Wilczek writes, "we change patterns of connections, secretions, and electrical impulses in our brains. To sense the world, we transform incoming patterns of electromagnetic radiation (sight), air pressure (hearing), local chemistry (taste and smell), and a few other data streams into that common brain currency."[24]

This is the sense in which the great philosopher Henri Bergson conceived of the human project. Our temporal lives, he wrote, afford us a blank canvas for what he called simply, "elaboration." Our existence in time is "a vehicle of creation and choice." As "artisans of our life, even artists when we so desire, we work continually . . . to mold a figure unique, original, unforeseeable as the form given by the sculptor to the clay."[25] The philosopher Max Scheler attacks this same problem: the uniqueness of the human in contrast to mere creatures. Every animal, he writes, "is securely embedded in the frame and *boundary of its environment*." We, by contrast, enjoy a "world-openness," the freedom to create, imagine, discover. "Only the human being is able to *soar* far above his status as a living being and, from a center above the spatio-temporal world, make *everything* the object of his knowledge."[26]

Marilynne Robinson considers that "no other species could be called ambitious" in this way, "determined to reshape the world beyond the modest sufficiency that satisfies the niche-finding and nest-building generality of creatures." With this creative freedom, error is an inevitable part of the package. In fact, "error," she continues, "is . . . an extravagance parsimonious nature . . . lavishes on us unstintingly."[27]

It may take some imagination to see in the human capacity for error the evidence of a divine gift. However, such room for error is intrinsic, not merely incidental. As the biologist Lewis Thomas points out, "The capacity to blunder slightly is the real marvel of DNA. Without this special attribute, we would still be anaerobic bacteria and there would be no music. . . . It is no accident at all that random mutations occur; the molecule of DNA was ordained from the beginning to make small mistakes."[28] Robinson marvels that "out of this indeterminacy, this great latitude, and within it, we construct our minds and our civilizations. These are things to be wondered at, certainly."[29] That we make so many mistakes within the orbit of that freedom is to her mind the evidence of an "extravagant" gift, an "indeterminacy, this great latitude."[30] No finer evidence could be found that we are here to learn, to experiment, to venture forth, and yes, to err. That word may be more apropos "when you remember," Gould adds, "that [error] came from an old root meaning to wander about, looking for something."[31]

These may sound like lofty abstractions, but the fact is such examples are clear indications that we are *fitted for* something more than the forty-hour work week, in the language of Abraham Maslow. Few of us set out daily and deliberately to fulfill the highest and noblest designs we are capable of conceiving; at the same time, we do live in dread terror, conscious or not, of uselessness, of plateauing, of boredom, of inutility. We are driven not just to *find* meaning or to *discover* meaning—but to *live meaningfully*. Those are incredibly revealing psychological facts. They explain why the essential tenor of so many lives is distraction, entertainment, business—anything as an alternative to the uselessness we sometimes fear our lives to embody. Consider what the actual experience of boredom signifies. It is doubtful (though possible) that animals experience boredom in the same way that humans do. They may suffer from lack of stimulation, from lack of activity, from confinement. But boredom? If we define boredom as a painful absence of desire or motivation—a piercing sense of purposelessness, then we describe a uniquely human affliction.

Scheler urges us to consider the inadequacy of materialistic, physical accounts of our identity. He writes, "The essence of the human being . . . encompasses, in addition to the thinking of ideas, a specific type of an 'intuition,' . . . and it encompasses also a specific class of volitional and emotive acts such as kindness, love, repentance, awe, states of wonder." What all these acts and states have in common, he continues, is our freedom to act in response to knowledge rather than environment, to values rather than instincts. An essential restlessness is our curse and our gift. The human "is never at peace with his environing world: he is always eager to break through the borders of now-here-whatness, always desirous to *transcend* the reality surrounding him." We can say no to our drives in pursuit of building something higher and better.[32]

I find all these conversations meaningful for the reinforcement they offer to the Restoration narrative of eternally existing souls, placed on earth for the purpose of fulfilling an embryonic potential to become like the gods who preside over this universe. It seems also striking that at this moment in Christian history, many notable theologians are reexamining the stories their traditions have been telling and are seeking more satisfying narratives. One of the most popular writers from *within* Christian tradition has noted that "some of our great controversies may have more to do with fresh interpretative schemes introduced at a later date than with the original meaning of the Bible" and that we must "restore" an earlier "vision" of the "ultimate future" God has in store for the human family. We must also, he writes, rexamine the critical question, "what we are saved *for*."[33] An Oxford Protestant theologian agrees that "Christianity is only now re-examining these alternative views of the future," involving "more constructive approaches to divine power and its interplay with humanity."[34] Multitudes of hearts are crying out for religion that is not just more nourishing but more rationally palatable. Themes that were once central elements of a Christian gospel—those of human freedom and possibilities open to an eternal, preexistent soul; of mortality as a school of love; of God as a parental tutor—disappeared from the tradition.

An eminent scholar in early Christian studies identified the fatal misdirection that occurred early in Christian history. Pelagius was a fourth-century cleric who wrote in defense of human free will. "We are not burdened by original sin," he taught.³⁵ And so our free will operates in cooperation with God's grace. Origen was a third-century church father who taught of the preexistence of the human soul, its inherent free will, the educative purpose of mortality, and a heaven capacious enough to embrace us all. Both Pelagius and Origen were condemned, and their teachings—once held to be orthodox—were anathematized as heresies. Elizabeth Clarke insightfully wrote that the church's twin condemnation of Pelagius and Origen ensured the triumph "of a Christian theology whose central concerns were human sinfulness, not human potentiality; divine determination, not human freedom and responsibility; God's mystery, not God's justice. Christianity was perhaps poorer for their suppression."³⁶

Another scholar notes that the Western Christian tradition got its historical form when "Augustine [built] original sin and its transmission, infant baptism, grace and predestination into a coherent theological system, while carrying the first and the last of these to extremes hitherto inconceivable."³⁷ Elaine Pagels made similar observations. "Christian converts of the first three centuries . . . regarded the proclamation of αὐτεξουσία—the moral freedom to rule oneself—as virtually synonymous with 'the gospel.'" Yet by the fifth century, "the message changed." More specifically, what "the majority of . . . Jewish and Christian predecessors . . . had read for centuries as a story of human freedom [the story of Adam and Eve] became . . . a story of human bondage."³⁸

It is at this point that we can draw together the insights of Abraham Maslow and scholar/theologians like N. T. Wright, Elizabeth Clark, and Elaine Pagels. What are we fitted *for*? In the story the Restoration tells, we are neither the collateral damage of a calamitous Fall, nor the product of biological happenstance. Our identity—and role in an eternal family—is not reducible to "a social construct or the product of evolution," as Elder D. Todd Christofferson writes.³⁹ "We are [God's] children," said George. Q. Cannon, "the children of Deity, with deity and godlike aspirations within us."⁴⁰

Restoration teachings do not just validate the eternity and irreducibility of human intelligence; they also encompass the entirety of human spirits in a vision of limitless opportunity and progress. One of the crowning aspects of the Restoration framework is its vast inclusiveness. According to Joseph Smith's teaching, "*All* the minds and spirits that god ever sent into the world are susceptible of enlargement and improvement."[41] Observers wonder at the peculiar practice of performing temple sacraments on behalf of the dead—ancestors and strangers alike. But few can dispute the vision such a practice proclaims to the world: in Joseph's words, "God will ferret out every soul that can be saved."[42] In the Latter-day Saint conception, the contingencies of history and circumstance are no impediment to the impulse, of God and of Saint, to extend the program of universal growth and progress and glory to every human being. Nor is the veil of death a barrier, as temple practice and descriptions of continuing labors in the postmortal world declare. Nikolai Berdyaev spoke with unknowing echoes of the beauty of Restoration doctrine when he wrote that the truly "'good' do not condemn the 'wicked' to hell and enjoy their own triumph, but descend with Christ into hell in order to free them."[43] Any conception of God that limits His love to a fortunate few beneficiaries of historical accident is a moral and rational nonstarter. As an author asked in the fourth century, "Shall then those be wholly deprived of the kingdom who have died before His coming?"[44]

The program of vicarious sacraments for the dead is not merely a final piece in the Restoration's totalizing vision of a comprehensive love; the interdependence it illustrates and enacts literalizes the human role as cocreators with God of human destinies. It is a response to the query anticipated by Berdyaev: "Moral consciousness began with God's question, 'Cain, where is thy brother Abel?' It will end with another question on the part of God: 'Abel, where is thy brother Cain?'"[45]

The view is common that faith is just mental entrenchment

in the face of contrary evidence. It can morph into such stubbornness. However, the history of the Restoration exemplifies an opposite conception of faith. As one of America's preeminent religious scholars notes (whether with approval or dismay is not fully clear), Joseph Smith's revelations lead to "realms of doctrine unimagined in traditional Christian theology."[46] Catholic scholar Stephen Webb was also struck by the substantial differences: "Of all the branches of Christianity, Mormonism is the most imaginative, and if nothing else, its intellectual audacity should make it the most exciting conversational partner for traditional Christians for the twenty-first century."[47] Clearly, the kind of faith practiced by Joseph Smith, and embedded in his inspired leaps of theological insight, was born of openness and wonder, not dogmatism and preconceptions. The practice of faith requires a stance of humility, of perpetual wonder and self-correction. Faith in the Restoration does not find, and is unlikely to ever find, philosophical or scientific proof. Nevertheless, the Restoration account of God, the human soul, and human destinies, finds resonance with principles of moral goodness and justice, of our deepest and noblest aspirations and yearning, and of intellectual reasonableness.

CHAPTER 6

SCRIPTURE

A turn toward a more rigorous approach to biblical scripture launched the modernist crises in Catholic and Protestant faith in the early twentieth century. Although the repercussions were felt in the institutional Church of Jesus Christ of Latter-day Saints in the 1930s, Restoration scriptural theology has a resilience traceable to Joseph's early and repeated comments about the historical forces at work in scriptural transmission. Although the Book of Mormon debates (and their Book of Abraham counterparts) continue unabated, rational grounds for faith in the Latter-day Saint canon are fully intact. That still leaves a lingering question: how can the prophetic voice be both fallible and reliable?

Historians generally trace the rise of secularism to the Enlightenment, that eighteenth-century intellectual movement that reconstituted philosophy on the basis of reason rather than tradition and authority. The growth of modern science, the spread of religious freedom, and a broader access to education made it increasingly safe—and even respectable—to raise new challenges to religious belief. A primary focus became the scriptural canon itself. "God" was a concept sufficiently amorphous, broad, and elastic to absorb any number of challenges; the Bible, however, made very specific claims about the earth's creation, Christ's divinity, and miraculous events.

And so the Bible became the fulcrum on which the competing claims of belief and unbelief inevitably came to focus. With the nineteenth century, a particularly devastating blow came with the rise of modern geological science. It was not Charles Darwin but Charles Lyell whose work forced a crisis in biblical Christianity. (It is important at this juncture to point out that, ironically, such developments would not have precipitated a crisis in the centuries before the Protestant Reformation.)

A Little Background on Scriptural Interpretation

Philo of Alexandria, a Jewish contemporary of Jesus, wrote extensively on the Hebrew scriptures. He read them through the lens of allegorical understanding, taking them as divinely inspired but as harboring a deeper truth than their literal meaning. In one example, he read the coat of skins in Genesis as an allegorical reference to the embodiment of premortal spirits as they enter this life. Origen was emphatic that the words of scripture were not always to be taken literally. Regarding those descriptions of the divine nature and divine actions that were inconsistent with what we know to be true of God, he urged: "We should be recalled to the search for that truth demanding a loftier and more diligent examination, and should eagerly search for a sense worthy of God in the Scriptures that we believe to be inspired by God."[1] A few centuries later, the most influential Christian after Paul, Augustine of Hippo, prayed to the Lord, "Grant me to hear and understand what is meant by *In the beginning You made heaven and earth.* . . . Were [Moses] here, I should lay hold of him and ask him."[2] Later, Augustine of Hippo would stipulate as a foundational principle of scriptural interpretation, "Whatever appears in the divine Word that cannot, when taken literally, be referred either to purity of life or soundness of doctrine, you may set down as figurative."[3]

This is not to say that any one of these individuals—or any one of their interpretations—should have authority for Christians or Latter-day Saints. It *is* to say that for much of Christian history, believing the Bible to be the word of God was a very different thing from the later belief in the Bible as a literal rendering of Creation, of history, or of anything else for that matter. In such a case, who then decides how to interpret scripture, what we are to understand literally, and what we are to understand morally or metaphorically or figuratively? "The church" was the simple answer for fifteen centuries. The authority of the church to declare doctrine and interpret scripture went largely (though not entirely) unchallenged for so long because (1) Bibles were expensive and rarely available to common folk, (2) literacy was not widespread among nonclergy, (3) even the literate and many of the clergy were not competent in the biblical languages or the Latin translation used by the church, and (4) the church was an institution that could not safely be opposed.

When the Reformation got off the ground in earnest with Martin Luther, what he saw as the laxness with which the church used and interpreted scripture was front and center in his criticisms. In fact, the very first two sentences of the famous ninety-five theses he posted on Wittenberg Church make this clear: "1. When our Lord and Master Jesus Christ said, 'Repent' (Mt 4:17), he willed the entire life of believers to be one of repentance. 2. This word cannot be understood as referring to the sacrament of penance, that is, confession and satisfaction, as administered by the clergy." Luther was disputing, in other words, the church's official interpretation of the biblical term *metanoeite*, which the Catholic translation (the Vulgate) rendered as *poenitentiam agite*, "do penance." Luther ended up rejecting five of the Catholic sacraments on this same basis—that the Bible cannot be interpreted in such a way as to justify them.

A pillar of all Reformation thought was that the Bible, and not the church, was the ultimate religious authority. So fundamental was this new understanding that the Westminster Confession—the most influential creed in Protestantism—makes it the subject of its very first article: "Of the Holy Scripture." There it is affirmed that the Bible is "infallible" and "immediately inspired." The qualifier "immediately" signifies "without intermediary or intervening agency."[4] In Luther's view, "the Holy Ghost is the all-simplest writer that is in heaven or earth; therefore his words can have no more than one simplest sense, which we call the scriptural or literal meaning."[5] That is to say, God's word is unaltered in the act of transmission, by the humanity of the author or the cultural milieu in which it occurs. The scriptures are furthermore declared to be "clearly propounded," "infallibl[y] tru[e]," "kept pure in all ages," and interpreted, if doubtful, only "by other places [in scripture] that speak more clearly."[6]

With a modern sensibility, we might well question just what scriptural "truth" means. Philo and Origen and Augustine and countless others in pre-Reformation Christianity thought the Bible "true." However, the Reformation emphasis on an unmediated and uninterpreted fullness of biblical truth was generally taken to mean that the words of the Bible were historically and scientifically, as well as morally true. Hence, the scholar and bishop of the Church of Ireland, James Ussher (1581–1656) felt confident in using the Bible's genealogical tables, supported by historical data, to compute the date of Creation—precisely—to October 23, 4004 BC. (The Cambridge scholar and churchman John Lightfoot was sure Ussher was off by a few decades; 3929 BC was his conclusion). Today we may smile condescendingly at such naivety, not to say audacity. My point, however, is that these rigid standards of biblical literalism and inerrancy were not the norm in historical Christianity—and they were not seconded by Joseph Smith or modern revelation.

Latter-day Saint Scriptural Interpretation

A visitor to a Latter-day Saint Sunday School class would often likely conclude that the Saints are "inerrantists," believing every word to be inspired, accurate, and true. As early as 1881, Apostle George Q. Cannon warned Saints against the error of thinking of the Bible "as infallible," as Catholics thought the Pope.[7] Many biblical inconsistencies and contradictions are patently impossible to reconcile. God is not a man that He should "change his mind," we read in Numbers 23:19 (NRSV). But a few books later, Jeremiah insists that if the people repent, "the Lord will change his mind" (Jeremiah 26:13, NRSV). Jehoiachin was eighteen years old when he began to reign according to one chronicler, but eight years old according to another.[8] Jesus hosts the Last Supper the first day of Passover, according to Matthew, Mark, and Luke. The day after, according to John. Judas hangs himself in Matthew, but he falls headlong and dies in Acts. And so on.

Joseph Smith taught as an article of faith that the source of inspiration is perfect, but the scriptural product is not always translated—or transmitted—correctly (Articles of Faith 1:8). Many Christians subscribe to the "Chicago Statement in Biblical Inerrancy," which leaves absolutely no room for the human factor: "Being wholly and verbally God-given, Scripture is without error or fault in all its teaching . . . in what it states about God's acts in creation, about the events of world history, and about its own literary origins under God." Furthermore, "the whole of Scripture and all its parts, down to the very words of the original, were given by divine inspiration."[9] That last phrase seems particularly problematic, since we don't even *have* the original words—what we have are copies of copies of copies of accounts of original words, letters, chronicles, and writings. The oldest manuscript of the Old Testament comes from almost two thousand years after Isaiah lived, and the oldest complete New Testament manuscript is dated to hundreds of years after Christ. And countless thousands of variations can be found in the myriad manuscripts in the biblical past. Even one supposedly standard translation, the King James Version, went through five different editions before Joseph Smith's lifetime, and more since.

Even if the stream of historical transmission were unadulterated and accurate, not every event or prophecy or revelation transmitted through human agents was a perfect expression of God's intent. Speaking *as* one of those prophet, seers, and revelators, George Q. Cannon wanted Church members to know that "the revelation we may get [is] imperfect at times because of our fallen condition and because of our failure to comprehend the nature of it. . . . Why? Because of *our* imperfection."[10] One author of scripture readily admitted the possibility of error in the New World canon of scripture. "If there are faults," Moroni wrote on the title page of the Book of Mormon, "they are the mistakes of men."

One photograph says more about the imperfect process of scriptural reception and formation espoused by Latter-day Saints than any number of sermons. Figure 7 is a transcript from one of the manuscript books into which Joseph Smith's scribes recorded his revelations. In introducing a volume of the Joseph Smith Papers, a Church website explains that these "revelation books" "preserve the earliest known copies of most of Smith's early revelations, and they are the key sources available for understanding the process of publishing the early revelations. The transcripts in this volume reproduce the original manuscripts of those books with great care, preserving corrections and revisions of any kind. Since *several scribes penned revisions in the manuscripts*, the handwriting of each scribe is rendered in a different color to facilitate analysis."[11]

This is an astonishing revelation of itself; Joseph, an oracle of God, prophet, seer, and revelator, enlisted the assistance of "several scribes" who "penned revisions" to his revelations. That they were openly invited to do so, and that the Church publishes the actual insertions and edits and changes they made, annihilates any mythology of all revelation as a matter of God dictating His words verbatim while a listening prophet recorded them perfectly, letter by letter, syllable by syllable. As Joseph elsewhere described revelation, "I will tell you in your mind and in your heart, by the Holy Ghost, which shall come upon you and which shall dwell in your heart. Now, behold, this is the spirit of revelation." And then the description ties Joseph Smith's process to that of biblical prophets who preceded him: "Behold, this is the spirit by which Moses brought

down from god in heaven with his garments; yea,
from the regions which are not knowing, clothed in his glorious
apparel, traveling in the greatness of his strength? I
shall say, I am he in righteousness, mighty to save.
& the Lord shall be red in his apparel, & his garments like him that treadeth in the wine vat & so
great shall be the glory of his presence, that the sun
shall hide his face in shame; & the moon shall withhold its
light; and & the stars shall be hurrelled from their places
and his voice shall be heard, I have trodden the
winepress alone, & have brought judgement upon all
people; & none were with me; & I have trampelled
them in my fury, & I did tread upon them in mine
anger; & their blood have I sprinkled upon my garments
and I have stained all my raiment; for this was the day
of vengeance which was in my heart, & now the year
of my redeemed is come, & they shall mention the loving
kindness of their Lord & all that he hath bestowed upon
them, according to his goodness, & according to his loving
kindness, forever & ever, in all their afflictions he was afflicted
& the angel of his presence saved them; & in his love, & in
his pity, he redeemed them, & he bare them & carried
them all the days of old; yea, & Enoch also, & they who
were with him; the prophets that were before him
& Noah also, & they who were before him, also Moses also
& they who were before him, & from Moses to Elijah
& from Elijah to John, who were with Christ in his
resurrection, & the Holy Apostles, with Abraham, Isaac,
& Jacob, shall be in the presence of the Lamb, & the graves
of the saints shall be opened, & they shall come forth & stand
on the right hand of the Lamb, when he shall stand upon
mount Zion, & upon the Holy City, the new Jerusalem,
& they shall sing the song of the Lamb day & night for ever
& ever. — & for this cause, that men might be partakers
of the glories which were to be revealed, the Lord sent forth the
fullness of his gospel, his everlasting covenant,

[recto]

REVELATION BOOK 1
3 November 1831 [D&C 133]

               died
¹⁶⁸down from god in heavn with ~~thy~~ garments; yea,
          which are
from the regions ~~that is~~ not known, clothed in his glorious
                        ²⁷
appearl, travling in the greatness of his strength? & he
    say,   who spake¹⁶⁹
shall ~~speak~~ I am me, be in righteousness, mighty to save.

& the Lord shall {re\be} read ~~read~~ in his appearl, & his garm
                             vat
=ents like him that treadeth in the wine ~~path~~ {&\&} so

great shall be the glory {in\of} his presence, that the Sun
                           with hold its
shall hide his face in shame; & the moon shall ~~be~~
light;
~~blown out~~ & the Stars shall be hurrelled from their place
     ²⁸
~~sockets~~ & his voice shall be heard. I have trodden the place¹⁷⁰
                            vat press
wine ~~press~~¹⁷¹ alone, & have brought Judgement upon all
             were
people; & none ~~was~~ with me; & I have trampelled

them in my fury, & I did tread upon them in mine

anger{;\,} & {0\their} blood have I sprinkeled upon my garme

-nts, & ~~have~~ stained all my r{0\(a)}iment: for this was the day
                             ²⁹
of vengeance which was in my heart. & now the year

of my redeemed is come, & they shall mention the loveing
                           has
kindness of their Lord; & all that he ~~hath~~ bestowed upon

them, according to his goodness, & according to his loving

kindness, forever & ever; in all their affliction he was afflicted.
³⁰
& the angel of his presenc[e] saved them; & in his love, & in
                         he
his pity, he redeemed them, & ~~did~~ bear them & ~~did~~ carr{y\ied}

them all the days of old; yea, & Enoch also, & they ~~which~~
                                 who
                              that
were with him; the Prophe{ts\rs} ~~which~~ were before him,
              who   Moses
& Noah also, & they ~~which~~ were before him,◊¹⁷² {0\&}; ~~Elijah~~ also
    who   Mosses Elijah,
& they ~~which~~ were before him, & from ~~Elijah to Moses~~
            Elijah
& from ~~Moses~~ to John, who were with Christ in his

resurrection, & the Holy Apostles, with Abraham, Isaac
                                 ³¹
& Jacob, shall be in the presenc[e] of the lamb.¹⁷³ & the graves

of the saints shall be opened, & they shall come forth & stand

on the right hand of the Lamb,¹⁷⁴ when he shall stand upon
                                  l
mount Zion, & upon the Ho{l\y} City, the New Jerusalem, ~~wherefo~~

& they shall sing the Song of the lamb day & night for ever
     ³²   made
& ever.— & for this cause, that men might be partakers
                           to be
of the glories which ~~were revealed~~ the Lord sent forth the
         his   his
fullness of ~~the~~ gospel, ~~& the~~ everlasting covenant.

ORIGINAL INSCRIPTION
John Whitmer

REVISIONS
Oliver Cowdery
William W. Phelps
Sidney Rigdon
Joseph Smith
John Whitmer
Unidentified

267. The stem of the "9" is visible, but the rest of the numeral is missing because the corner of the leaf is torn.

268. This leaf, containing manuscript pages 119–120, was removed from the manuscript book at some point and is located at the Community of Christ Library-Archives.

269. Or "spoke".

270. "place" was inserted on the wrong line and then stricken. Because the edge of the leaf worn, the line endings are obscured, and both this insertion and the inserted "place" one line above may be "places".

271. Two layers of deletion: first layer by Sidney Rigdon and second layer by John Whitmer.

272. "◊" likely a punctuation mark.

273. Triple underlining beneath "I" wipe-erased.

274. "b" possibly retraced by a later scribe.

Figure 7: Pages from The Joseph Smith Papers, Revelations and Translations: Manuscript Revelation Books, Facsimile Edition, *showing edits from four colleagues (see Doctrine and Covenants 133).*

the children of Israel through the Red Sea on dry ground" (Doctrine and Covenants 8:3).

This Latter-day Saint conception of scripture is a far cry from the position of other Christians—and of some Latter-day Saints unfamiliar with these backgrounds—who wish to force scripture and prophets into a marbled perfection with no place for human limitations. Our faith—our mental and spiritual lives—would be easier if we had such a golden calf of infallibility to adore, but we do not. The reality makes our mortality an inescapable risk; we are compelled to be free, with an ever-present burden of responsibility.

Another scriptural challenge is that for many moderns, and Latter-day Saints in particular, scriptural language of judgment, anger, and retribution can seem overly harsh and inconsistent with the Jesus of the New Testament and the weeping God of Moses 7. For many of the rising generation (and older!), threats and terror are not only ineffective but also more prone to repel than invite. It is useful in such cases to keep a few considerations in mind. First, consider the virtual impossibility of employing a fluid language that is resonant with all peoples, in all societies and contexts, across a spectrum of moral development and centuries of cultural evolution. We all tend to suffer from "presentism," the tendency to make judgments and evaluations through the lens of our own particular moment in history.

We condemn—rightly—the evils of the past, judging according to the light of our own day and our own conscience. However, we may miss two points that presentism often ignores: (1) We may ourselves have done no better if subjected to the same historical and individual disadvantages of those we judge in past eras. (2) More pertinent to our own situation, we may forget that not all societal developments are healthy ones (such as many fruits of the sexual revolution: abortion, single parenthood, and the commodification of sexual intimacy generally); but on the whole, it is clear that as a people, humans have made enormous progress. As a rule, we recognize the evils of slavery, racism, child labor, imperialism and wars of conquest, cruelty to animals, and the enforced subservience of women. We don't execute for stealing a handkerchief, and we don't torture suspected heretics (although, undoubtedly, our descendants will blanch at some of our own moral blind spots).

But here is the lesson from those examples: such practices were commonplace from biblical times to as late as the nineteenth century (and beyond). Brutality, indifference to human suffering and dignity, violence, and oppression have been dominant features of our civilizations and most others. Is it not apparent that language appropriate to such hardness of heart was fittingly employed to break through human imperviousness to the light of Christ? The Lord indicates as much, when He explains that the specter of an "eternal" punishment is not to be taken literally but is employed "that it might work upon the hearts of the children of men" (Doctrine and Covenants 19:7). That statement—in the voice of God—should be sufficient to answer the perennial question, Why does the language of scripture, including the Book of Mormon, seem at times so out of harmony with a tender, loving, long-suffering God?

The point is reinforced in the preface to the Doctrine and Covenants when we are told that the Lord speaks to us "in [our] weakness, after the manner of [our] language" (1:24). Brigham Young took this to mean that the Bible and Book of Mormon alike, if rewritten by an angel in the nineteenth century (let alone the twenty-first) "would in many places be very different from what it now is."[12] It is a simple fact that in Latter-day Saint understanding, scriptural language is influenced by the needs and sensibility of the immediate audience on the one hand, and by the intellectual and cultural prism of those composing it on the other. We should not expect, for example, that language directed to ancient peoples who practiced the human sacrifice of children (as alluded to in Deuteronomy), augmented by cannibalism (in the Book of Mormon), should in every instance sound pleasing and conformable to the sensibilities of average Saints dwelling in twenty-first-century American suburbia or modern Chile or Mongolia, struggling their best to live gospel standards.

How can we treat the Bible as the inspired word of God if it is, as the Church affirms on its website, not "without error"?[13] The difficulty is beautifully addressed in a Jewish analogy:

> How can you distinguish the word of God from other, ordinary, human words in Scripture? I do not know of any litmus test that can be used. I suppose I have my suspicions about this verse or that one, but I really do not believe it is my business to try to second-guess the text's divine inspiration. And so, I like to think about Scripture in the same terms I think about the Temple Mount in Jerusalem. That little flat-topped, squared-off hill (a short walk from my house) was once the site of Solomon's temple, and then, after that temple was destroyed by the Babylonians, it soon became the site of the second temple, until it too was put to the torch, this time by the Romans. It lay in ruins for several centuries, until the Muslim conquest of Jerusalem, when the Dome of the Rock and the al-Aqsa mosque were built on it. . . . Custom and, eventually rabbinical decree forbade pious Jews from ascending that hill and walking about, lest by accident their foot defile the place where once the Holy of Holies stood, the place of God's presence on earth. . . . This prohibition is in force to this day. So every day, pious Muslims and Christian pilgrims and Japanese tourists climb up the steps and walk all around the Temple Mount, but religious Jews do not. . . . I have my own ideas about where the Holy of Holies once stood. . . . So couldn't I just walk very carefully around on the outer perimeter and stand there, safe in the knowledge that I am not violating the space once occupied by God's presence? But of course, I don't. I like to think of Scripture as a similar sort of space. I certainly could not pinpoint Scripture's Holy of Holies, the very center from which the divine presence radiated outward. . . . It is all one sacred precinct; indeed, the divine presence suffuses every part of it."[14]

Latter-day Saints have additional aids in reading scripture both faithfully and intelligently. The Book of Mormon and modern revelation affirm the uninspired changes that have entered into the biblical record ("plain and precious things" lost and "interpolations by the hands of men" [1 Nephi 13; Doctrine and Covenants 91:2]); Joseph produced an inspired revision to the Bible, and Parley Pratt drew an insightful analogy that prophets have affirmed. In Pratt's example, "Scriptures resulted from a revelatory process and are thus the product of revealed truth, not the other way around. . . . People would do well to look to a stream for nourishing water, but do better to secure the fountain."[15] In other words, to believe in God is to believe in a living, speaking God. To consider scripture more authoritative than the Spirit that prompted it is to get things exactly backwards. That was Joseph's point: "Some will say, the scriptures say so & so," he told a large congregation with some impatience. But "I have the oldest Book in the world [the Bible] & the Holy Ghost I thank God for the old Book but more for the Holy Ghost."[16] "The Holy Ghost is the infallible testimony to the Believer," affirmed Wilford Woodruff.[17] Pratt's point has been reaffirmed by two living Apostles. "What makes us different from most other Christians," said President Dallin H. Oaks, "in the way we read and use the Bible and other scriptures, is our belief in continuing revelation. For us, the scriptures are not the ultimate source of knowledge. . . . The ultimate knowledge comes by revelation."[18] And Elder Jeffrey R. Holland echoed: "The scriptures are not the ultimate source of knowledge for Latter-day Saints. They are manifestations of the ultimate source. The ultimate source of knowledge and authority for a Latter-day Saint is the living God. The communication of those gifts comes from God as living, vibrant, divine revelation."[19]

Searching requires both effort and discernment. It may truthfully be said of Christ that He was "of no apparent beauty,"[20] for the realities of the invisible world are not for the casual observer. But Christ's beauty was abundantly manifest to those with discerning hearts and eyes. So may we all discern His voice in the scriptures if we seek to hear it. Through the Spirit we may find the sometimes-hidden God, the one who knows us by name, who weeps with us in our pain, and who has graven us on the palms of His hands.

Costly Discipleship

Some challenges we find in the scriptures are not reducible to imperfect intermediaries or troubling language calibrated to "work upon the hearts of the children of men" (Doctrine and Covenants 19:7). As we read the scriptures with discernment, disciples do not shy away from the "hard things" the scriptures need to communicate to us. We are beings inherently constituted to become something that we have not yet become: to love in ways we do not yet love, to be wise in ways that we are not yet wise, and to be good in ways we are not yet good. If this is true, then the gulf that separates the self as I now am from the self I am in process of becoming is one that can only invite fearful resistance or anxious engagement. At least, that is so to the extent that I am aware of that gulf and am beckoned to traverse it. It is in *this* sense—of religion as a summons to a more abundant life—that the scriptural template will generally *not* comport with a therapeutic age that is often more concerned to reconcile us to what we are than to beckon us toward what we might become.

All this is to say, discipleship is costly, and at some point in the journey, the scriptural template that beckons and incites and cajoles will *not* be one that feels comfortable or comforting. As David Bentley Hart notes, "Throughout the history of the church, Christians have keenly desired to believe that the New Testament affirms the kind of people they are, rather than—as is actually the case—the kind of people they are not."[21] The point must finely but firmly be understood: the scriptures are clear on the inflexibility of those characteristics and virtues that constitute a holy and celestial life. But the scriptures also affirm the tirelessness of a Healer, who "is

SCRIPTURE

patient with you, not wanting any to perish" (2 Peter 3:9, NRSV). Or as He said through Isaiah, "For I the Lord thy God will hold thy right hand, saying unto thee, fear not: I will help thee" (Isaiah 41:13).

CHAPTER 7

THE "NEW MORMON HISTORY"[1]

For Latter-day Saints, the greatest contests between faith and intellect have played out on the field of our Church history. Like many assaults on faith, the burgeoning attacks on the Church's historical narrative in the internet age resulted in many positive developments. Our history was enhanced by more professionalism and accuracy, it was made more accessible to a wide audience, and it provoked a more nuanced and reflective engagement with the underpinnings of our faith. The winnowing of belief, separating the essential ground of faith from its cultural overlays, is a painful but essential process in the life of discipleship.

A Presbyterian Sunday School curriculum is unlikely to spend alternating years rehearsing the life of John Calvin and the story of the Reformation. Nor do Lutherans sing hymns to Luther or devote lesson manuals to the suppression, two decades before Haun's Mill, of the orthodox Lutherans in Germany.[2] Why does our history rise to the level of formal church instruction on Sundays, and why does Joseph Smith loom larger for Latter-day Saints than comparable figures in other Christian faith traditions? And more importantly, do the benefits of these practices outweigh the costs?

The answer to these questions derives from the role of authority and truth claims as they are founded in the Christian religion. Catholicism bases its status as the authorized church of Jesus Christ on its understanding that Jesus personally vested Peter with the keys to act in His name. And that authority passed to subsequent Popes by direct succession. The paradigm shifted dramatically with the rise of Protestantism. Martin Luther and John Calvin and John Wesley all pointed their followers to the Bible as the ground of authority and salvation. Scripture, not apostolic succession or direct anointing, was the basis of their religious enterprises. The Bible itself is the supreme source of ecclesiastical truth and doctrine in Protestantism.

At the remove of two centuries, it is easy for us to miss one of the most remarkable of Joseph Smith's earliest claims. The entire possibility of a Christianity based on *sola scriptura* (scripture alone) is rendered incoherent in Joseph Smith's personal experience, which demonstrated the need for a divine commission behind the Restoration of the gospel of Jesus Christ. As Joseph recounts in his personal narrative, "Teachers of religion of the different sects understood the same passage of Scripture so differently as to destroy all confidence in settling the question [of religious truth] by an appeal to the Bible" (Joseph Smith–History 1:12). What may appear a simple description of his frustrated search for scriptural direction becomes, in light of what follows, evidence of the utter failure of the grand project of the Reformation. The great turn from apostolic authority to confidence in the Bible is utterly rejected by Joseph Smith on the basis of his personal experience but also on the ground of the historical record of Protestant fragmentation and endless schism. The Bible had proved insufficient. Hundreds of sects were, by virtue of their very existence, proof of the inadequacy of the Bible—or of the futility of institutional religion itself as the path to God.

At the center of this Christian fragmentation, contention, and disarray, one historian remarked, religious leaders had "darkened the human soul with the most absurd and blasphemous conception of God in all the long and honored history of nonsense."[3] A new beginning, a fresh start, a virtually complete erasure of the past and the reintroduction of the weeping God of Enoch, remade Christian possibilities. A boy and his prayer for spiritual healing[4] was the human lens through which the divine light pierced the veil, and a wholesale Restoration was launched.

Joseph's story is told and retold in the Church, not because his character was flawless or his life story is inherently deserving of scriptural status. Rather, the reality of his visionary encounters constitutes the facticity of God's reentry into human history in the same way that the original apostolic witnesses are the foundation of the Resurrection as a historical event. In both cases, one would be mistaken if one assumed that the person (Peter or John or Joseph) was more qualified by virtue of their individual character or attributes than for the role they were called to occupy as a special witness and revealer of truth. That is why the Restored Church places an emphasis—unusual in the Christian world—on the experiences of that individual through whom authority and truth are presented to the world with refreshing clarity and power.

So how important is the historical narrative we tell about the Restoration? And what details matter? Before answering this question, it may be useful to revisit the first crisis that erupted in the New Testament church. The question that ruptured the communion of the Jerusalem Saints was straightforward: was circumcision necessary for the Gentile converts to the faith? Most religious questions presuppose larger principles and assumptions. In this case, the larger question implied was "What practices are *essential* to the Christian life?" Circumcision, it turns out, was not. To require it, would be to impose "a yoke upon the neck of the disciples" that was irrelevant to gospel living (Acts 15:10). Ironically, then, the lesson learned was that over-belief can be as much of a problem as under-belief. Some elements of religious essentials inevitably become indistinguishable from cultural practice. At times, it is necessary for the practicing disciple to reexamine her spiritual convictions and winnow the chaff from the kernels, the contingent from the nonnegotiable.

History matters. Not just because the origins of the Restoration are rooted in historical claims—but because *all* Christian faith is ultimately founded in the veracity of pivotal events that really took place in time and space. Was Jesus raised in Nazareth or Bethlehem? Was He born in 6 BC or 4 BC according to our calendar? Was His birth in a traveler's inn or a shepherd's cave? These may be no more than idle questions. But *that* He was born as a human babe, of divine parentage in the meridian of time, cannot be disputed without turning faith into fairy tale.

The most important event in the history of the universe occurred when the spirit of the eternal Christ reanimated the remains of a crucified body, inaugurating a universal resurrection that will enfold the faithful, His deniers, and every reader of this book. That moment in an ancient dawn registered palpably on whatever sundial or water clock in a royal palace marked the minutes. The meaning of that Easter morn is transcendent, its repercussions eternal; but it happened on a particular dawn as constellations that will never again have the same alignment in the night sky faded, as shopkeepers prepared their wares in the market amid conversations never to be repeated, and while birds bred and eggs hatched whose atoms have long since dispersed—the moments that marked the rising of Christ were as historical and real and as much a part of our universe as the seconds that pass as you read these pages. To render that event when time turned a corner as allegorical, metaphorical, or just comforting fiction—as skeptics and liberal theologians alike have done—is to make the Christian faith into a pathetic delusion masquerading as sublime hope.

So to repeat: history matters—in the sense that those events that make our faith efficacious, transformative, and redemptive must be grounded in the world of flesh and bone and spirit. Peter's denial of Christ does not impede His healing power. Three wise men or many do not determine the divinity of the child they worshipped, and a forbidden apple or a forbidden pomegranate does not touch on the destinies at stake in Eve's decision to eat. We need to apply the same standard to Restoration history. In *what* are we proclaiming faith, exactly? Where is the locus of the "power of godliness" that is being asserted (Doctrine and Covenants 84:20)? One answer appears in a consistent motif remarked upon by observers of early Christians. Christian scholar Marcelo D'Ambrosio goes straight to the heart of Christian faith: speaking of the first generation of disciples who died for their religion, he wrote that "Ignatius and his fellow martyrs died for a person, not an ideology."[5] Their faith was *manifest* in their belief in, and loyalty to, that person whose life and mission had impressed upon them the power of an absolute, transformative love. And that love was amplified and spread by the prism of their discipleship. Their manifest love for one another made Christ present to multitudes.

A third-century chronicler noted this of the new religion: "Christians showed unbounded love and loyalty, never sparing themselves and thinking only of one another. Heedless of danger, they took charge of the sick, attending to their every need and ministering to them in Christ, and with them departed this life serenely happy; for they were infected by others with the disease, drawing on themselves the sickness of their neighbors and cheerfully accepting their pains. Many, in nursing and curing others, transferred their death to themselves and died in their stead."[6] The catalyst for such unparalleled selflessness was the introduction into cultural currency of the belief in a God whose compassion and self-sacrifice knew no bounds.

The most prominent critic of the era found the absolute, universal love of this God utterly bewildering: "The Christian God is apparently moved by feelings of pity and compassion for the sort of men that hang about the Christian churches, or so at least they believe." And then he concluded in disdain, "Well, what do we have in the end? An impressive god indeed:

one who desires nothing more than to adopt sinners as his children; one who takes to himself the creatures who stand condemned by another, the poor wretches who are (as they say of themselves), naught but dung."[7]

Such conceptions of God and the reach of His love did not survive the fifth century. Author Tom Holland has written of a "distinctively Christian understanding of love" that has been at times "cut loose from its theological moorings."[8] Today, major Christian voices from the Protestants to the Catholics to the Orthodox, from N. T. Wright to Richard Rohr and Brian McLaren and David Bentley Hart recognize that something, somewhere, went off the rails long ago. N. T. Wright laments that too many contemporary Christian views are "a basically paganized vision" of divine "wrath," and "with that failure many other things have been lost as well."[9] Richard Rohr and Brian McLaren write that "we in the West gradually lost this profound understanding of how God had been liberating and loving all that is. Instead, we gradually limited the divine presence. We might say that the door of faith closed on the broadest and most beautiful manifestation of the incarnation."[10] And David Bentley Hart refers to "ennobling fragments of the ruined edifice of the old Christendom"—an "inexhaustible source" from which we need to "draw renewed vigor" and "imagine new expressions of the love it is supposed to proclaim to the world."[11]

The operative questions for Saints are, did Joseph Smith or did he not experience firsthand the unspeakable love of a living God, and did he do three things: Did he reconstitute a fuller, more accurate description of that living God? Did he articulate a more coherent saga of human origins and destinies? And did he bring into the present the theology and possibility of rendering more durable and holy our relationships to each other and the heavenly family? Or we could for the sake of simplicity—and of urgency—boil those questions down to one: *Does our Restoration faith make God more present to us and to the world?*

The facts, the details, the stories that matter are all embedded in *that* question. This isn't to say the facts and details and stories don't matter. It *is* to say the revelation or nonrevelation of God's presence in our lives tells us all we need to know about the path that took us there. It affirms that the "plain and precious things" (1 Nephi 13:29) were in fact repaired and reinstated. Don't find yourself asking someone else's questions, with someone else's motivations. John recounts a time when disciples deserted the Christ for a variety of reasons and concerns that pervaded the community of new believers. Did Jesus really preach that men had to literally drink His blood? Did He have the authority to promise literal immortality? Did He offer a sustenance superior to the manna delivered through Moses? Was the will of the Father truly a limiting factor in their hopes of salvation? Was His allegation of pending betrayal true? All these questions troubled His followers. Those who stayed did so because of the answer they experienced to the only question that mattered. Was He who He said He was? "Thou hast the words of eternal life. . . . Thou are that Christ, the son of the living God" (John 6:50–66). God had been made present to them.

Before he even accepted baptism in the new faith, Brigham Young encountered the same barrage of questions some are still asking about the Restoration. But those questions were not his question. "The doctrine [Joseph] teaches is all I know about the matter, bring anything against that if you can. As to anything else I do not care, . . . for I never embrace any man in my faith. But the doctrine he has produced will save you and me, and the whole world; and if you can find fault with that, find it."[12]

How does the Restoration provide the conditions for us to taste the salvific reality of Christ? Abundant routes are possible. It may be in the story of Joseph's First Vision, which serves as master template for our own Sacred Grove experience, inspiring us to go and do likewise. It may be in the way Joseph made literal and concrete the ancient dream of Zion, organizing us into those exasperating and sanctifying schools of love we call wards and branches. For some, it is the provocative portrait of a God who mourns with us and through us and over us in our pain, shattering our inherited illusions about His indifference or distance. Or it may be the whole package of encounters with the divine that enshroud us in the warp and woof of God's continuing accessibility—from Lehi's theophanies to Joseph and Sidney's shared sojourn into celestial worlds down to the holy presence we approach in personal temple worship. In these or comparable stories is the test of the Restoration saga's veracity. Austin Farrer, a cobeliever in the Christ we worship, wisely wrote, "I shall not call my faith in doubt, for since God has shown to me a ray of his goodness, I cannot doubt him on the ground that someone has made up some new logical puzzles about him. It is too late in the day to tell me that God does not exist, the God with whom I have so long conversed, and whom I have seen active in several men [and women] of real sanctity."[13]

CHAPTER 8

THE POVERTY OF SECULARISM

The history of religion—and Christianity in particular—is decidedly mixed. Dogma, persecution, racism, and inequality seem endemic in institutional religion. Isn't the environment most conducive of freedom, independent thought, and social progress to be found outside the walls of formal religious structures? Or could our confidence in the resources of a secular world be misplaced?

The Restoration interpretation of what transpired in Eden is remarkable in modern Christianity. The Saints believe that Eve should receive "reverent honor" and "encomiums of praise" for her decision to partake of the tree of knowledge, made in deference to the higher of two competing demands—replenish the earth and abstain from the fruit.[1] Terribly important in this regard is the recognition that Eve was justifiably drawn to characteristics of the fruit: it was "good," it was "pleasant to the eyes," and it was "desired to make one wise." The Good, the Beautiful, and the True beckoned, and by partaking, Eve and Adam "bec[a]me as one of [the Gods]" (Genesis 3:6, 22).

Absent faith in the wellsprings of our own eternal souls, oblivious to the educative and transformative designs behind our embodiment, and unresponsive to the call of an absolute love, how do humans fare in the pursuit of Truth, Goodness, and Beauty? By way of response, I take as just one category of illustration a puzzle occupying some of the greatest minds of contemporary thought: how to account for the presence of human life in the universe in the face of astronomically high odds against the possibility.

By any reasonable standard, far too many improbable conditions are necessary for life to thrive, for our existence to be the result of chance. Martin Rees, the astronomer royal of Great Britain, writes of a half dozen of the most impressive. As just one example, he points to the value referred to as ε (epsilon), which is a measure of the nuclear binding force that holds the nucleus of atoms together. It has a value of 0.007. If it were 0.006, there would be no other elements; if it were 0.008, then protons would have fused in the big bang, leaving no hydrogen to fuel future stars. Or take Q, which is the one-part-in-100,000 ratio between the rest mass energy of matter and the force of gravity. If this ratio were even fractionally smaller, there could have emerged no stellar material for planetary formation. A wee bit larger, all stars would collapse into black holes.

Rees is convinced that the odds of a whole array of such conditions existing by chance is not just unlikely; they are statistically, wildly improbable, effectively impossible given the universe's duration of only billions of years. And that is without even considering the dozens of "coincidences" necessary for life as we know it to exist on this planet: a moon to create tidal waves and stabilize the earth's orbital angle, creating regular seasons; a liquid outer core to produce a protective magnetic field; nearby superplanets to absorb most threatening meteoroids; a position in the galaxy that shields us from cosmic radiation; and so forth. Rees concludes that to account for the emergence of this planet that nourishes and sustains human life, only two explanations are conceivable. In the first, an intelligent Creator has a role in this thriving, brimming planet—and our presence on it. With admirable honesty, Rees declares simply: "If one doesn't accept the 'providence' argument [which he doesn't], there is another perspective which . . .

I find compellingly attractive. It is . . . an infinite multiverse."[2] If only an infinite number of universes can produce a scenario that is statistically impossible, then infinite universes there must be. Of course, one need not be a scientist to recognize that such a desperate—and unprovable—hypothesis sounds less like science and more like that very leap of faith he shuns.[3]

A school of theoretical physicists has posited a similar claim, called the "many world" interpretation of quantum physics. The arguments are quite complex, but they grow out of the early twentieth-century discovery that depending on how one performs a given act of measurement, a beam of light will manifest as either a wave or as particles. Subsequent experiments have suggested that at the subatomic realm, cause and effect break down, matter exists only as "probability waves," and reality comes into being only when it is observed.

Rather than sacrifice principles that have long undergirded science and common sense alike—that reality exists independent of our observing it and that matter acts according to law in predictable ways—some scientists have explained the puzzles of subatomic behavior by asserting that "this universe is constantly splitting into a stupendous number of branches, all resulting from the measurement-like interactions between its myriads of components. Moreover, every quantum transition taking place on every star, in every galaxy, in every remote corner of the universe is splitting our local world on earth into myriads of copies of itself."[4] It should be noted at this point that not only is such a hypothesis uncomfortable to rational sensibility, but it would reduce individual life to utter meaninglessness. As one of its proponents concedes, "There is no wrong decision, for—in [this] view—there exists a universe in which" every conceivable decision is simultaneously made.[5] No decision you make, no action you take, could in this scheme of things matter at all.

One needn't be an astronomer or a physicist to recognize a few key points from the state of contemporary thinking about the nature of reality. The world we inhabit, the universe in all its majesty and beauty, is far more complex, and far more mysterious, than we believed in the aftermath of Isaac Newton. What is now clear is the dawning awareness that we *cannot* make sense of the universe in the ways we have always thought we could. Three-dimensional representations of subatomic reality are not even possible. ("Any attempt to visualize the behavior of the microscopic, subatomic entities makes a mockery of our intuition," notes one physicist.)[6] Most striking of all, some cutting-edge hypotheses like the above parallel the faith foundations of religion (a multiverse is neither provable nor falsifiable), but they do not propose explanations for our existence that preserve purpose, meaning, or moral significance to the human condition.

One doesn't—or shouldn't—choose a paradigm because it comports with how one wishes the world to be. One chooses a system of belief, whether in multiverses, atheism, or Restoration Christianity, because it provides the best explanations for the most questions of greatest concern. In my view, such a master framework should encompass the three matters of greatest value to humans:

1. Does it satisfy my yearning for truth and understanding? Does my belief system feed that hunger, enrich my store of knowledge, and provide the tools and resources and incentives to propel me further in the quest? Is it broad and generous and daring enough to plumb the secrets of the real universe, which contains such diverse realities as mosses and stellar clusters, along with Mother Teresas and Shakespeares?

2. Does it satisfy my yearning for the beautiful? The most influential scientist of the modern era, Charles Darwin, opened a door to one world, but unintentionally shut it on another. He wrote,

> My mind seems to have become a kind of machine for grinding general laws out of large collections of facts, but why this should have caused the atrophy of that part of the brain alone, on which the higher tastes depend, I cannot conceive. A man with a mind more highly organised or

better constituted than mine, would not I suppose have thus suffered; and if I had to live my life again I would have made a rule to read some poetry and listen to some music at least once every week; for perhaps the parts of my brain now atrophied could thus have been kept active through use. The loss of these tastes is a loss of happiness, and may possibly be injurious to the intellect, and more probably to the moral character, by enfeebling the emotional part of our nature.[7]

I want a standard for my life that valorizes science and mathematics, while being expansive and robust enough to recognize the incompleteness of those apprehensions of reality that do not see the beautiful as mere adornment, pastime, or sentimental indulgence—but as indispensable nourishment to my soul.

3. Does it satisfy my yearning for the good? George Santayana wrote that "beauty is the sensible manifestation of the Good,"[8] and Ralph Waldo Emerson said music and poetry "are not satisfactions, but suggestions."[9] Restoration teachings do more than alert us to the Divine's attribute and gift of moral goodness; the gospel that weaves the imitation of Christ into our destiny, teaches us how to embrace, to emulate, and to be restored to the presence of that Divinity. Our innate recognition of the good does not easily translate into our enactment of the good.

Grounded in truth, prompted by the beautiful, and schooled and disciplined in the good, I see the gospel as offering the same fruit that appealed to Eve, and for the same reasons. In that magnificent story of human beginnings, the parents of the race knowingly embark on a costly, painful, expansive, and educative sojourn into mortality as the only route to the good, the beautiful, and the wisdom that the fruit—unleashing embodiment and experience—represent.

Our yearning for truth, beauty, and goodness is universal. But our attempts to find them outside of a comprehensive framework are scattershot and often unsatisfying. In 2021, the *New York Times* reported the peculiar specter of an atheist's election as chief chaplain of Harvard. Subsequent media commentary ranged from outrage to resignation, but amid the controversy one fact is clear: the irrepressible yearning for "spiritual" fulfillment in the absence of organized religion leads to many ironies and absurdities. A chaplain who operates outside of religious categories or a commitment to a God of any sort is an irrepressible manifestation of a hunger that draws us beyond the strictly material and mundane. Yet the quest for spirituality, without a community in which to practice love and long-suffering, tends toward self-concern and sterility. We crave a larger narrative that gives meaning to our scattered intimations of beauty and peace and to the form and purpose of one's life. Spirituality without religious commitment reminds one of the character in a novel by V. S. Naipaul: she had several opinions, but in the collective they did not "add up to a point of view."[10]

CONCLUSION

> *Seeing revelation as a synthesis of knowledge that comes to the "heart" and to the "mind" (Doctrine and Covenants 8:2) is one of the great contributions of the Restoration. The Lord's invitation to "reason together" is but one of many indications that our grasp of eternal verities can be aided by rational discussion. This book does not resolve all tensions or answer all the challenges that thoughtful individuals may encounter, but it has demonstrated that the life of discipleship can sustain—and it can grow—through honest engagement with honest questions.*

Einstein was certainly one of the greatest scientists of the modern era. In his opinion, the greatest logician of the last two thousand years was his contemporary, the mathematician Kurt Gödel. His principal contribution, the 1931 incompleteness theorem, is hard for nonspecialists to follow in detail. In essence, he demonstrated that in any given logical system—such as mathematics—there will be statements that are impossible to prove using just that system's axioms. There are truths, in another formulation, that are simply not provable—even mathematical ones that we know to be true.[1] Widely considered the most significant twentieth-century theorem in mathematics, the implications have been controversial for exactly what they reveal about the limits of knowledge.

For Gödel himself, his theorem confirmed his earlier

intuition that "there were truths to be found not just in the empirically perceivable, but perhaps more beautiful and enduring ones in the realm of abstract conceptions, where they awaited human discovery [but] not through tangible perception." In his biographer's words, he was awake to "the astonishing fruitfulness of human intuition." He "firmly believed that his proof was profoundly encouraging for human creativity. Humans will always be able to recognize some truths through intuition . . . that can never be established even by the most advanced computing machine. . . . In place of limits on human knowledge and certainty, he saw only the irreplaceable uniqueness of the human spirit."

But did those intuitions extend to credible assurance about the reality of God and eternal beings? "It was to be expected after all that my proof would be made useful for religion sooner or later," he wrote his mother. And such inferences, he added, were "doubtlessly supportable."[2]

"In the end, only kindness matters." Or so sings the songstress Jewel. Not a bad sentiment, that, and not a bad start. Kindness—replicating the divine propensity for affirming the worth and beauty of other human beings, and promoting their thriving, is perhaps the most meaningful virtue we can pursue. However, a great many things besides kindness will matter in the end: Loyalty to loved ones. Courage to stand up for the oppressed and marginalized. Living one's life with integrity. Serving others. To live a rich and abundant life, the circle must spread even wider: Gratitude for the grandeur of nature. The capacity to appreciate a beautiful melody. Cheerfulness in the face of disappointment. A sense of humor that dulls the edge of pain and enhances the joy of friendship. Curiosity that stretches the mind and immunizes the soul against boredom and stasis.

And what about truth? Does truth matter? If faith without works is dead, knowledge without wisdom is dangerous, and truth without charity is sterile. As part of the abundant life, and as an essential catalyst to both happiness and growth, certainly truth is indispensable. And the more of it we can recognize, the greater our satisfactions. We can enjoy Beethoven without knowing how to read music; we can love the stars in complete ignorance of astrophysics; and we can be a good neighbor without knowledge of either God or our own origins. But she who reads music will see patterns and hear motifs of which others are blind and deaf; he who knows a red giant from a hot blue sees variety and history where others see no more than a featureless variation of light; and those who perceive the reality of heavenly parents, or an eternal past, and of an educative purpose in our mortality just may find the catalyst they need to persevere in affliction, find genuine connection with the divine, and cooperate more joyfully in the project of building communities of ever-larger scope and longer duration.

It may be true, as Marx opined, that religion can be an opiate, an anesthetic. It may be the case, as the ancients cynically remarked, that humans create some gods in their own image. And it is certainly a fact, as legions of professional and amateur therapists alike have claimed, that religion can be a refuge, a retreat from reality. It is, in the words of one theologian, beyond dispute that "those who put their faith in God do so for all sorts of good reasons. The very best reason," he continues, "is that they are finally, utterly, and incontrovertibly convinced that the faith in which they put their confidence is *true*."[3] That may be so. But for all of us, as Elder Jeffrey Holland stated, "belief [is] always the first step toward conviction." And "belief is a precious word," for which one "never need apologize."[4]

A theology professor relates that a student, disappointed with her grade, asked what she could do to improve on the next exam. "Become a deeper person," the teacher responded.[5] The words might have stung, but there may be no gentler way to make the point: we are only as deep as the questions we are asking—and there are no shortcuts. "The things of God are of deep import; and time, and experience, and careful and ponderous and solemn thoughts can only find them out," said

Joseph Smith. "Thy mind, O man! if thou wilt lead a soul unto salvation, must stretch as high as the utmost heavens, and search into and contemplate the darkest abyss, and the broad expanse of eternity."[6]

Galileo, the greatest mind of his era, wrote to a friend, "I have always felt so unable to understand what light is that I would gladly have spent all my life in jail, fed with bread and water, if only I was assured that I would eventually attain that longed-for understanding."[7] The fourteenth-century mystic Julian of Norwich experienced a series of thirteen visions as a young woman. She spent twenty years in an anchorite's cell—two full decades of her life walled off from the world in solitary austerity—determined to fully fathom the religious truths embedded in those transcendent experiences. The result was one of the greatest explorations of the love of God ever written, a chronicle of the certainty she had experienced that "there is no being made who can know how much and how sweetly and how tenderly our Maker loves us."[8]

The nineteenth-century cleric Edward Beecher was

Figure 8. Galileo, by Justus Sustermans

Figure 10. Depiction of a bishop blessing an anchoress, ca. 1400. From a manuscript held by Corpus Christi College, Cambridge

Figure 9. Statue of Julian of Norwich by David Holgate, outside Norwich Cathedral

determined to crack the mystery of God's justice. His brother described the price he paid to find understanding of the doctrine of premortal existence: "None but those most intimate with the author, most acquainted with his habits of prayer, and deep humiliation before God, & entire consecration to Christ can form any idea of the travail of soul which [he experienced]. Many hours he lay prostrate on his face before God agonizing in prayer for the holy spirit. One felt in entering his study at such times as Moses felt when the voice said 'Put off thy shoe from thy foot for the place whereon thou standest is holy ground.'"[9]

Discipleship and scholarship both demand the sweat and toil of staying with a question. Shallow sound bites do not just infect the media; the façade of erudition and worldliness can be just as prevalent. Our Western intellectual heritage is magnificent and worthy of celebration—but it also teaches caution and hesitancy and humility. The earth-centered cosmos died in the seventeenth-century, witch burning in the eighteenth,

CONCLUSION

Figure 11. Edward Beecher

and bloodletting by leeches and belief in spontaneous generation in the nineteenth, while ice-pick lobotomists won Nobel Prizes in the twentieth. Each age is confident it has reached the end of historical development, but each generation's ignorance is pitied condescendingly scant decades later. Which of our age's paradigms about human nature, educational psychology, economic systems, medical practice, and political theory will embarrass our grandchildren? Marilynne Robinson notes that many of our "systems and ideologies, however we might embroider them, are in effect simple and simplifying—the invisible hand, the survival of the fittest, the dictatorship of the proletariat, superego, ego, and id. They are the antibiotics of the intellect, killing off a various ecology of reflection and experience in order to eliminate one or two troublesome ideas."[10] What "antibiotics of the intellect" threaten, and how might we cultivate our own "ecologies of reflection"?

It should not go without notice that in the Gospel of Mark, Christ takes potential disciples, subjects of His healing and instruction, "apart into a desert place," "aside from the multitude," or "out of the town" (Mark 6:31; 7:33; 8:22–23). Few things in life are harder than to extricate ourselves from the preconceptions, the intellectual world, or the culture into which we are born and raised. The dream of liberal humanism, like that of the Romantics and of America's founders, emphasized a radiant human intellect—one that, elevated above the tempests of history and the fog of culture, could shape its own destiny and that of humanity by recognizing and responding to transcendent truths and values. One key to the abundant life I have tried to limn is simple—or not so simple—attentiveness. To live one minute is to be immersed in manifold sensations like an exposed nerve. To live a decade is to begin the slow descent into recognition, reiteration, automatic response, and habituated patterns of thought and action.

Medical researcher Druin Burch makes an alarming comparison in this regard. Commenting on the propensity of dead pheasants to litter the roadsides in the UK, he writes, "The frequency with which a driver on a rural English road hits a pheasant is a cultural phenomenon, and the culture responsible is partly that belonging to the pheasant. . . . Their response to cars, from trying to run ahead of them to bolting onto the road when one approaches, is part inborn stupidity but part cultural ignorance." What he means is that pheasants are "reared en masse to be shot."[11] That is what they are acculturated, bred, artificially selected *for*. If they were originally created for another end, it was bred out of them. Which takes us back to the question with which we began. What are *we* fitted *for*? We, too, are shaped—and misshaped—by culture. The hypnotic delusions of the market, the media, the cult of celebrity, and the passion for popularity are more potent than the military industrial complex (cigarettes, as shorthand evidence of that fact, have killed more humans than all the devastation of two world wars[12]).

The power of culture is greater than we can begin to appreciate. An evolutionary biologist has studied how "culture can and does alter our brains, hormones, and anatomy, along with our perceptions, motivations, personalities, emotions, and many other aspects of our minds."[13] Nonetheless, one contemporary philosopher observes that we all recognize our personal growth over time, and positive change involves the acquisition of values we did not at one time possess—values that are not culturally determined. "In accounting for the genesis of our new values, we often have occasion to mention the effects on us of forces outside our control. . . . But [such influences] do not fashion us. We have a hand in answering the question as to what things in the world are important to us, and our answers need not be, and typically are not, random or arbitrary. Agency, as distinct from mere behavior, is marked by practical rationality. . . . Becoming someone is something someone *does*, and not merely something that happens."[14]

In 1794, the German philosopher Fichte arrived at the University of Jena and addressed the student body on the topic of "the vocation of man." He believed that anyone engaging in the pursuit or promulgation of knowledge needed to begin with the same question with which we began this book: What are we *for*? What is our true vocation, consistent with our true nature? His answer: to be something better than we at present are, to engage our hearts and minds in the project of self-transformation. "Perfection is the highest unattainable end of man," he said, "whilst eternal perfecting is his vocation. He exists, that he may become ever morally better himself, and make all around him physically, and . . . morally better also."[15]

One contemporary neuroscientist writes that "reason is arguably the highest achievement of the human brain."[16] That reflects a pretty impoverished view of our species and sells short, in tragic fashion, the most noble and praiseworthy achievements. Ancient Rome produced aqueducts and cement and Cicero—a host of monuments to human intellect. But what caused the Romans to marvel was behavior that defied, rather than reflected, reason. One scholar describes conditions during the second century's horrific epidemic, "known as the Plague of Galen (165–180), in which hundreds of thousands of people died in the streets." The onslaught revealed, according to Cyprian of Carthage, "whether the well care for the sick, whether relatives dutifully love their kinsfolk as they should, whether masters show compassion for their ailing slaves, whether physicians do not desert the afflicted." At the height of the disaster, "Christians stayed behind in plague-ravaged cities while others fled. Their acts of mercy extended to all the suffering regardless of class, tribe, or religion."[17] When asked her opinion of the first sign of human civilization, Margaret Mead reportedly said it was prehistoric human remains showing a healed femur.[18] Compassion for the helpless was evident long before the first technology. Super colliders are impressive, but are they more reflective of humankind at its best than orphanages and Doctors Without Borders?

The question is not just one of moral betterment; an expansive, inquiring, and curious mind is also inseparable from an infinite capacity for joy that is divine in nature. Bertrand Russell had the seeds of this insight but did not apprehend the fruit: "There is no abstract and impersonal proof either that strawberries are good or that they are not good. To the man who likes them they are good; to the man who dislikes them they are not. But the man who likes them has a pleasure which the other does not have; to that extent his life is more enjoyable and he is better adapted to the world in which both must live. . . . The more things a man is interested in, the more opportunities of happiness he has."[19] Intellectual and moral activity, rather than beatific contemplation, are the essence of the heaven to which Latter-day Saints aspire. "Whatever principle of intelligence we attain unto in this life, it will rise with us in the resurrection." Adding a prod to the promise, the Lord continued, "And if a person gains more knowledge and intelligence in this life through his diligence and obedience than another, he will have so much the advantage in the world to come" (Doctrine and Covenants 130:19).

To those who struggle to persist in the quest for understanding, in the face of doubts and perplexities, the words of Einstein may be particularly apt. "It is not that I am so smart. But I stay with the questions much longer."[20] Sometimes, the cost of staying with the question is high. But the cost of abandoning the quest is higher. "What terrible torments this thirst to believe has cost me and still costs me," wrote the novelist Fyodor Dostoevsky, "becoming stronger in my soul, the more there is in me of contrary reasonings. And yet sometimes God sends me moments in which I am utterly at peace."[21]

EPILOGUE

*"All the confusion is for want of
drinking another draught."*
—Joseph Smith

I was about twelve years old. My father invited me to come along for one of his monthly visits to a run-down shop that sold used books. He was a distant father for the most part. No baseball games or family picnics or playing catch in the yard. So I always ran to the car on these occasions before he changed his mind. I could pick something out for myself, he said as he hunted through the stacks and overflowing boxes on the floor. I remember distinctly picking one, then two, then a third, and maybe a fourth. History, science, adventure stories—the titles I have long since forgotten. Then, as he made his own purchases, I stood and looked around at the beckoning worlds beyond number represented by the myriad volumes. One called to me and then another. A paltry selection gathered in my arms, a puny island set against the immense seas that receded in all directions. I remember vividly the next moment, when I returned all the books to the shelves and went to the car, despondent and defeated by the impossibility of it all.

In visits yet to come, I relented and gradually acquired the foundations of a considerable library. At times the old hopelessness descends even now. At other times, I run my hand along the bookcases and retrieve a volume acquired decades ago, never opened until this moment. And I marvel anew at how fresh and alive a voice sounds, that so patiently waited

EPILOGUE

Figure 12. Trinity College Library

in quiet neglect over the passing years. The poet Shelley was humbled by the false pride of the ancient king Ozymandias, whose achievements disintegrated beneath the sands of time, leaving only the ruins of a pretentious epigraph.[1] I find a library both more daunting and more hopeful in that regard. Sometimes, a single sentence can fill me with a holy envy and holy pride both, for the tongue of angels with which members of my human species have spoken ("that flesh is but the glass that holds the dust, that measures all our time"[2]). Other times, an economical insight of power is the ice pick to break the frozen sea of my mind ("There must be much in our teaching of Christianity and our living of it which is at fault, if good [people] react in total disbelief of it"[3]). Some passages are so densely woven that I feel like a child abandoned by the mentors of my youth, before my education prepared me for the conversation of the aged and wise ("Conviction in the moral sense signifies being conquered, vanquished, in our active nature by an ideal end; it signifies . . . the authority of an ideal over choice and conduct"[4]).

And in works of natural history, I can again be a child seeing the world for the first time. (Did you know that the human body occupies a place in the spatial world exactly halfway between subatomic and stellar objects? Or that some people are born with four color receptors instead of three, allowing them to see ninety-nine million more colors than you?) Biographies offer sweet consolation for the finitude of my own life, so narrowly circumscribed to one brief span in one small orbit of friends and experience, and historical narratives give me some respite from the claustrophobia of presentism, with its convenient amnesias and pretensions to moral finality.

I conclude with these reflections because ultimately, my personal journey has been one that cannot tease out the workings of faith and reason, intellect and spirit. As with the essayist Emerson, the great works of human creativity have been to me suggestions of something more eternal. I resonate with the experience attested by Robert Frost; in exposing oneself to the monuments of the human mind, one "can tell the moment it strikes him that he has taken an immortal wound—that he will never get over it."[5] These experiences may be what Wordsworth had in mind in writing about

> Those obstinate questionings
> Of sense and outward things,
> Fallings from us, vanishings;
> Blank misgivings of a Creature
> Moving about in worlds not realized.[6]

Faith, in my conception, is not a silencing of the intellect. It is the only path by which the fullest appetites of the intellect find satisfaction.

FURTHER READING

Barlow, Philip L. *A Thoughtful Faith: Essays on Belief by Mormon Scholars.* Moscow, ID: Canon Press, 1986.

    Barlow, himself a leading thinker and writer in the contemporary Church of Jesus Christ, compiled some twenty essays by leading Latter-day Saint scholars across a variety of disciplines who found a synthesis of faith and reason in their professional and spiritual lives.

England, Eugene. "Why the Church Is as True as the Gospel." The Eugene England Foundation. http://eugeneengland.org/wp-content/uploads/sbi/articles/1999_e_004.pdf; this was originally published in *Sunstone* 22, nos. 3/4 (June 1999): 61–69.

    In this classic essay by a gifted Latter-day Saint disciple and intellectual, England explains why the imperfections of the Church—and its members—are essential ingredients in the educative and sanctifying process we call mortality.

Givens, Terryl, and Fiona Givens. *The Crucible of Doubt: Reflections on the Quest for Faith.* Salt Lake City: Deseret Book, 2014.

    Many of those wrestling with their faith find their way hedged up by misleading assumptions and expectations regarding the Restoration. This book examines a number of problematic paradigms, from prophetic infallibility to risk-free faith.

Givens, Terryl, and Nathaniel Givens. *Into the Headwinds: Why*

Belief Is Hard and Always Has Been. Grand Rapids, MI: Eerdmans, 2022.

In this volume, Terryl and his social-science–trained son explore how recent developments in our understanding of human nature, cognition, and human psychology intersect with the nature of religious faith. Counterintuitively, they argue that secularism is not the problem. Headwinds have always assaulted believers from the days of the first apostles and are an inescapable part of the disciple's path.

Givens, Terryl. *Wrestling the Angel: The Foundations of Mormon Thought: God, Cosmos, Humanity*. New York: Oxford University Press, 2014.

This volume is a historical overview of Latter-day Saint theology, situating Restoration doctrines within—and against—the context of traditional Christian positions on the great and timeless questions. Topics covered include the origins of the soul, the nature of God, the purpose of life, and the destinies in store for humankind.

Madsen, Truman. *Eternal Man*. Salt Lake City: Deseret Book, 1990.

In this slim volume, one of the tradition's most beloved teachers and philosophers presents his reflections on six perennial challenges in philosophy, from the problem of evil to the nature of human freedom. In each case, he articulates the unique insights Restoration thought brings to bear.

Mason, Patrick. *Planted: Belief and Belonging in an Age of Doubt*. Salt Lake City: Deseret Book, 2015.

Mason, who holds the Leonard Arrington Chair of Mormon History and Culture, offers practical advice on how to stay rooted in the gospel while living in a secular age that challenges religious commitments in general and Restoration claims in particular.

Maxwell, Neal A. *Things as They Really Are*. Salt Lake City: Deseret Book, 1978.

FURTHER READING

Elder Maxwell, who spoke powerfully about the essential role in the Church of the "disciple scholar," here elaborates his vision of how the doctrines of the restored gospel provide a comprehensive framework for making sense of the world.

Swinburne, Richard. *Is There a God?* Oxford: Oxford University Press, 2010.

Swinburne, who was a fellow of the British Academy and Oxford philosopher, provides a succinct and readable argument that belief in God is necessary for a complete and compelling explanation behind the universe revealed through scientific discovery.

NOTES

Introduction

Chapter epigraph: "Elder Cook Speaks at Stanford on Knowledge, Faith, and Moral Values," *Church News*, October 28, 2015, https://www.churchofjesuschrist.org/church/news/elder-cook-speaks-at-stanford-on-knowledge-faith-and-moral-values?lang=eng.

1. Often attributed to Mark Twain, but probably apocryphal. See "The Apocryphal Twain," Center for Mark Twain Studies, https://marktwainstudies.com/the-apocryphal-twain-if-you-dont-read-the-newspaper-youre-uninformed-if-you-do-youre-misinformed/.
2. "A Closer Look at How Religious Restrictions Have Risen around the World," Pew Research Center, July 15, 2019, https://www.pewforum.org/2019/07/15/a-closer-look-at-how-religious-restrictions-have-risen-around-the-world/.
3. Few serious students of history, philosophy, or religion find anything remotely respectable in the arguments of leading New Atheist Richard Dawkins. Professor of historical theology at Oxford Alister McGrath, for instance, notes that Dawkins' *God Delusion* is "a work of theater rather than scholarship." And the leading Marxist intellectual and literary critic Terry Eagleton observes accurately that the whole school relies upon "a version of Christianity that only seriously weird types . . . would espouse." Alister McGrath and Joanna Collicutt McGrath, *The Dawkins Delusion?* (Downers Grove, IL: InterVarsity Press, 2007), 96; Terry Eagleton, *Reason, Faith and Revolution: Reflection on the God Debate* (New Haven: Yale University Press, 2009), 5.
4. John C. Lennox, *Can Science Explain Everything?* (Epson, England: Good Book, 2019), 17.
5. Rodney Stark, *For the Glory of God: How Monotheism Led to Reformations* (Princeton: Princeton University Press 2003), 194–95; "Faith and Reason," *The Economist*, February 22, 2014, 28.
6. Elaine Ecklund et al., "Religion among Scientists in International Context," *Socius* 2 (2016): 1–9, https://doi.org/10.1177/2378023116664353.
7. Jennifer Wiseman, cited in Anna Salleh, "Are Religion and Science Always at Odds?" ABC News, May 23, 2018, https://www.abc.net

NOTES

.au/news/science/2018-05-24/three-scientists-talk-about-how-their-faith-fits-with-their-work/9543772.

8. Quentin Smith, cited in William Lane Craig and J. P. Moreland, eds., *Blackwell Companion to Natural Theology* (Chichester, UK: Wiley-Blackwell, 2012), ix.
9. Stan L. Albrecht and Tim B. Heaton, "Secularization, Higher Education, and Religiosity," in *Latter-day Saint Social Life: Social Research on the LDS Church and Its Members*, ed. James T. Duke (Provo, UT: BYU Religious Studies Center, 1998); emphasis added.
10. Unless otherwise indicated, biblical citations are from the King James Version. Sometimes, the New Revised Standard Version (NRSV) is used for greater clarity or accuracy regarding the point being made.
11. Jonathan Haidt, "Religion, Evolution, and the Ecstasy of Self-Transcendence," TED Talk, March 14, 2012, https://www.youtube.com/watch?v=2MYsx6WArKY&ab_channel=TED.
12. Abraham H. Maslow, *A Theory of Human Motivation* (Eastford, CT: Martino, 2013), 15.
13. Michael Gazzaniga, *Human: The Science Behind What Makes Us Unique* (New York: HarperCollins, 2008), 7.
14. Cited in Philip Yancey, *Prayer* (Grand Rapids, MI: Zondervan, 2006), 24.
15. Hugh W. Nibley, "The Way of the Church," in *Mormonism and Early Christianity*, The Collected Works of Hugh Nibley, ed. Todd M. Compton and Stephen D. Ricks, (Salt Lake City: Deseret Book, 1987) 4:302–4.
16. Tom Stoppard, *Arcadia* (New York: Farrar, Straus and Giroux), 79.
17. Aristotle, *Metaphysics* I.1., trans. W.D. Ross, The Internet Classics Archive, MIT, http://classics.mit.edu/Aristotle/metaphysics.1.i.html.
18. Lowell L. Bennion, *How Can I Help? Final Selections by the Legendary Writer, Teacher, and Humanitarian* (Murray, UT: Aspen Books, 1996), 111.
19. Edmund Burke, *A Philosophical Enquiry into the Origin of Our Ideas of the Sublime and Beautiful* (Edinburgh: Cupar, 1821), 27.
20. See Charles Taylor, *A Secular Age* (Cambridge, MA: Harvard University Press, 2007).
21. Maslow, *Theory of Human Motivation*, 9.
22. G. K. Chesterton, *Orthodoxy* (Mineola, NY: Dover, 2004), 11.
23. G. K. Chesterton, *Collected Works* (San Francisco: Ignatius Press, 1986), vol. 34, 395.
24. The saying is ascribed to Bernard de Fontenelle and cited in Marcelo Gleiser, *The Island of Knowledge: The Limits of Science and the Search for Meaning* (New York: Basic Books, 2014), xx.
25. John Milton, *Paradise Lost*, book 8, ll, 167–77, in *The Complete Poetry and Essential Prose of John Milton*, ed. William Kerrigan, John Rumrich, and Stephen M. Fallon (New York: Modern Library, 2007), 502–3.
26. Guillermo Gonzalez and Jay W. Richards, *The Privileged Planet: How*

NOTES

Our Place in the Cosmos Is Designed for Discovery (Washington, DC: Regnery, 2020), 10.

27. Gonzalez and Richards, *Privileged Planet*, 151.
28. Lawrence M. Krauss, *A Universe from Nothing: Why There Is Something Rather than Nothing* (New York: Atria, 2012), 108.
29. Gleiser, *Island of Knowledge*, 92.
30. Albert Einstein, *Journal of the Franklin Institute*, 1936; cited in Andrew Robinson, "Did Einstein Really Say That?" *Nature* 557, no. 30 (April 30, 2018), https://www.nature.com/articles/d41586-018-05004-4.
31. Joseph B. Wirthlin, "Press On," general conference, October 2004, https://www.churchofjesuschrist.org/study/general-conference/2004/10/press-on?lang=eng.
32. Neal A. Maxwell, "The Inexhaustible Gospel," August 18, 1992, BYU Speeches, https://speeches.byu.edu/talks/neal-a-maxwell/inexhaustible-gospel/.

Chapter 1: Myths and Straw Men: Reason and Christian Beginnings

1. Robert Alter, *The Art of Biblical Poetry* (New York: Basic Books, 1986), 87; in Michael Austin, *Rereading Job: Understanding the Ancient World's Greatest Poem* (Salt Lake City: Kofford Books, 2016), 79.
2. He learns, as one rich example, that the moral law does not entail immediate reward or punishment (as his final condition illustrates), and, as another, that we should seek righteousness for the good it can do for others, not ourselves ("your wickedness affects others like you and your righteousness other human beings" [Job 35:8, NRSV]).
3. For one of many such dismissals, see Richard Dawkins, *A Devil's Chaplain: Reflections on Hope, Lies, Science, and Love* (Boston: Houghton Mifflin, 2003), 243.
4. Sam Harris, as paraphrased by Johann Hari in his review essay, "The End of Faith by Sam Harris: The Sea of Faith and Violence," *The Independent*, February 11, 2005, https://www.independent.co.uk/arts-entertainment/books/reviews/the-end-of-faith-by-sam-harris-745110.html.
5. "Historical Introduction to Philosophy/Faith and Reason," Wikiversity, https://en.wikiversity.org/wiki/Historical_Introduction_to_Philosophy/Faith_and_Reason.
6. A Google Books search reveals dozens and dozens of contemporary miscitations of this phrase.
7. Tertullian, *On the Flesh of Christ* 5, *Ante-Nicene Fathers* [*ANF*], ed. Alexander Roberts and James Donaldson (Peabody, MA: Hendrickson, 1995), 3:525.
8. From an excellent overview of the phrase's history by Peter Harrison, "'I Believe Because It Is Absurd': Christianity's First Meme," April 9, 2018, AEON, https://aeon.co/ideas/i-believe-because-it-is-absurd-christianitys-first-meme.

9. Tertullian, *Against Marcion* 5.1, *ANF* 3:429; Tertullian, *Repentance*, 1.1, *ANF* 3:657.
10. Tertullian, *The Prescription Against Heretics*, *ANF* 3:246.
11. Stephen Jay Gould, "Non-Overlapping Magisteria," in *The Richness of Life: The Essential Stephen Jay Gould*, ed. Steven Rose (New York: Norton, 2007,) 594.
12. Étienne Gilson, *Reason and Revelation in the Middle Ages* (Singapore: PIMS, 2020), 6–7.
13. As did the second-century philosopher Celsus, who mocked Christians for saying, "The wisdom of this life is bad, but that foolishness is a good thing!" See Origen, *Against Celsus* 1.9, in *ANF* 4:400.
14. Colin Brown. *Christianity and Western Thought: From the Ancient World to the Age of Enlightenment* (Downers Grove, IL: InterVarsity Press, 1990), 89–90. Brown is citing Justin Martyr, *First Apology* 5.46 and *Second Apology* 8.13.
15. Clement of Alexandria, *Stromata* 6.8, in *ANF* 2:495.
16. Marcellino D'Ambrosio, *When the Church Was Young: Voices of the Early Fathers* (Cincinnati: Servant Books, 2014), 86.
17. All citations from Jocelyn M. C. Toynbee, "Dictators and Philosophers in the First Century A.D.," *Greece & Rome* 13, nos, 38/39 (June 1944): 43–58.
18. Origen, *First Principles* 2.11.4, *ANF* 4:298.
19. Jacqueline Mariña, "Friedrich Schleiermacher and Rudolf Otto," *Oxford Handbook of Religion and Emotion*, ed. John Corrigan (New York: Oxford, 2016), 457.

Chapter 2: Inquisitions and Intellect in Christian History

1. Colin Brown. *Christianity and Western Thought: From the Ancient World to the Age of Enlightenment* (Downers Grove, IL: InterVarsity Press, 1990), 11.
2. Seb Falk, *The Light Ages: The Surprising Story of Medieval Science* (New York: Norton, 2020).
3. Mark Noll, "A. D. White's 'Warfare between Science and Theology,'" *Biologos*, August 7, 2010, https://biologos.org/articles/a-d-whites-warfare-between-science-and-theology.
4. Ronald L. Numbers, ed., *Galileo Goes to Jail and Other Myths about Science and Religion* (Cambridge: Harvard University Press, 2009), 1; emphasis in original.
5. Paul Feyerabend, *Against Method* (London: Verso, 2010), 128–29.
6. Craig A. Boyd, "The Synthesis of Reason and Faith," in *Faith and Reason: Three Views*, ed. Steve Wilkins (Downers Grove, IL: InterVarsity Press, 2014), 132.
7. Falk, *Light Ages*, 90.
8. Falk, *Light Ages*, 297.
9. Alfred W. Crosby, cited in Rodney Stark, *For the Glory of God: How Monotheism Led to Reformations, Science, Witch-Hunts, and the End of Slavery* (Princeton: Princeton University Press, 2003), 135.

NOTES

10. Stark, *For the Glory of God*, 63. Stark points out that Calvin did not actually take his position offered at Paris.
11. George Haven Putnam, *Books and Their Makers in the Middle Ages* (New York: Hillary House, 1962), 1:91.
12. A. F. Leach, *The Schools of Medieval England* (New York: Benjamin Blom, 1968), 1–2.
13. This is a partial list of the works enumerated by Alcuin in 780, at York. Putnam, *Books and Their Makers*, 1:108–9.
14. Putnam, *Books and Their Makers*, 1:viii–ix.
15. Charles Homer Haskins, *The Rise of Universities* (Ithaca: Cornell University Press, 1975), 24.
16. Henry Mosheim, *Ecclesiastical History* (London 1841), 2:529, quoted in John Henry Newman, *The Idea of the University* (New York: Doubleday, 1959), 62.
17. As Rodney Stark notes, "Classical learning did not provide an appropriate model for science." *For the Glory of God*, 134.
18. The University of Virginia was founded in 1819, the first nonreligious university in America.
19. Numbers, *Galileo Goes to Jail*, 1.
20. Ian F. McNeely and Lisa Wolverton, *Reinventing Knowledge: From Alexandria to the Internet* (New York: Norton, 2008), 85.
21. David Bentley Hart, *Atheist Delusions: The Christian Revolution and Its Fashionable Enemies* (New Haven: Yale University Press, 2009), 101.
22. Judge and Lewis both cited in John Lennox, *Can Science Explain Everything?* (Epsom: The Good Book Company, 2019), 18–19.
23. McNeely and Wolverton, *Reinventing Knowledge*, 39.
24. Falk, *Light Ages*, 78.
25. Falk, *Light Ages*, 82–83.
26. Hart, *Atheist Delusions*, 100.
27. "Religion, or Theology," *Encyclopedia Britannica* (Edinburgh: A. Bell and C. MacFarquhar, 1771), 2:533.
28. John Taylor, "The Knowledge of God," *Journal of Discourses* (Liverpool: Franklin D. Richards and Samuel W. Richards, 1851–86; rpt. Salt Lake City, 1974), 16:197.

Chapter 3: Heart and Mind United

1. Dean C. Jessee, ed., *The Papers of Joseph Smith, Volume 1: Autobiographical and Historical Writings* (Salt Lake City: Deseret Book, 1989), 1:357.
2. Manuscript History of the Church, A-1, 130, Church History Library, Sal Lake City; see also Larry C. Porter, "The Colesville Branch in Kaw Township, Jackson County, Missouri, 1831 to 1833," in *Regional Studies in Latter-day Saint Church History: Missouri*, ed. Arnold K. Garr and Clark V. Johnson (Provo, UT: Brigham Young University, 1994), 286–87.
3. *Elders' Journal* 1, no. 4 (August 1838): 53.

NOTES

4. Joseph Smith as cited in *The Words of Joseph Smith*, ed. Andrew F. Ehat and Lyndon W. Cook (Orem, UT: Grandin Book, 1991), 113–14.
5. Thomas Dick, *Philosophy of a Future State* (Philadelphia: Biddle, 1845), v, 136, 145, 166.
6. Stan Larson, "The King Follett Discourse: A Newly Amalgamated Text," *BYU Studies* 18, no. 2 (Winter 1978): 204.
7. *The Complete Discourses of Brigham Young*, ed. Richard S. Van Wagoner (Salt Lake City: Smith-Petit Foundation, 2009), 4:1972.
8. Larson, "King Follett Discourse," 202.
9. *Words of Joseph Smith*, 379.
10. *Complete Discourses of Brigham Young*, 3:1505.
11. *Complete Discourses of Brigham Young*, 5:2910.
12. Orson Pratt, "Concentration of the Mind," *Journal of Discourses*, 7:157.
13. Joseph Smith, journal, December 22, 1835, Manuscript History of the Church, B-1, 672, Church History Library, Salt Lake City.
14. James H. Eells to Br. Leavitt, Kirtland, Ohio, April 1, 1835, in *Among the Mormons: Historic Accounts by Contemporary Observers*, ed. William Mulder and A. Russell Mortensen (New York: Knopf, 1958), 88.
15. See *Improvement Era* 53, no. 12 (December 1950).
16. Thomas Alexander, *Things in Heaven and Earth: The Life and Times of Wilford Woodruff, A Mormon Prophet* (Salt Lake City: Signature Books, 1993), 41, 47.
17. Eliza R. Snow Smith, *Biography and Family Record of Lorenzo Snow* (Salt Lake City: Deseret News, 1884), 3.
18. Pearl Wilcox, *Latter Day Saints on the Missouri Frontier* (Independence, MO: n.p., 1972), 102.
19. See George Givens, *In Old Nauvoo: Everyday Life in the City of Joseph* (Salt Lake City: Deseret Book, 1990), 227–36.
20. Givens, *In Old Nauvoo*, 237, 242.
21. Givens, *In Old Nauvoo*, 242.
22. H. Dean Garrett, ed., *Regional Studies in Latter-day Saint History: Illinois* (Provo, UT: Department of Church History and Doctrine, 1995), 341.
23. Manuscript History of the Church, 1838–1856, C-1, 1145, Church History Library.
24. "Seventies' Library," *Times and Seasons* 5, no. 24 (1 January 1844): 763.
25. Kenneth W. Godfrey, "A Note on the Nauvoo Library and Literary Institute," *BYU Studies* 14 (Spring 1974): 386–89.
26. James R. Clark, comp., *Messages of the First Presidency of The Church of Jesus Christ of Latter-day Saints*, 6 vols. (Salt Lake City: Bookcraft, 1965–75), 1:323.
27. T. Edgar Lyon Jr., *John Lyon: The Life of a Pioneer Poet* (Provo, UT: BYU Religious Studies Center, 1989), 225.
28. B. H. Roberts, *The Autobiography of B. H. Roberts*, ed. Gary James Bergera (Salt Lake City: Signature Books, 1990): 54.

NOTES

29. Leonard J. Arrington and Davis Bitton, *The Mormon Experience* (New York: Random House, 1979), 337. "Projecting Bachelor Degree Recipients by Gender," *Postsecondary Opportunity* 102 (December 2000); Mabel Newcomer, *A Century of Higher Education for American Women* (New York: Harper & Brothers, 1959), 46.
30. Janath Russell Cannon, Jill Mulvay Derr, and Maureen Ursenbach Beecher, *Women of Covenant: The Story of Relief Society* (Salt Lake City: Deseret Book, 1992), 107.
31. See Claudia L. Bushman, *Mormon Sisters: Women in Early Utah* (Logan: Utah State University Press, 1997), 58–59.
32. Statistics quoted by Charles Ellis, a non–Latter-day Saint, in *Scrapbook of Mormon Literature* (n.p.: Ben Rich, n.d.) 2:151–52; ranking from *Contributor* 4, no. 5 (February 1883): 183.
33. Spencer W. Kimball, "The Second Century of Brigham Young University," October 10, 1975, BYU Speeches, https://speeches.byu.edu/talks/spencer-w-kimball/second-century-brigham-young-university/.
34. *Complete Discourses of Brigham Young*, 3:1477.
35. M. Russell Ballard, "The Opportunities and Responsibilities of CES Teachers in the 21st Century," An Evening with Elder M. Russell Ballard: Address to CES Religious Educators, Salt Lake Tabernacle, February 26, 2016, https://www.churchofjesuschrist.org/broadcasts/article/evening-with-a-general-authority/2016/02/the-opportunities-and-responsibilities-of-ces-teachers-in-the-21st-century?lang=eng.
36. Neil L. Andersen, "Faith Is Not by Chance, but by Choice," general conference, October 2015, https://www.churchofjesuschrist.org/study/general-conference/2015/10/faith-is-not-by-chance-but-by-choice?lang=eng.
37. Russell M. Nelson, "Where Is Wisdom?" general conference, October 1992, https://www.churchofjesuschrist.org/study/general-conference/1992/10/where-is-wisdom?lang=eng.

Chapter 4: The Problem of God, Good, and Evil

1. Os Guinness, *Time for Truth: Living Free in a World of Hype and Spin* (Grand Rapids, MI: Baker, 2006), 69–72.
2. John Calvin, *Institutes of the Christian Religion*, trans. Henry Beveridge (Peabody, MA: Hendrickson, 2008), 630.
3. Martin Luther, cited in Michael Massing, *Fatal Discord: Erasmus, Luther, and the Fight for the Western Mind* (New York: HarperCollins, 2018), 674.
4. J. Ellis McTaggart, *Some Dogmas of Religion* (London: Edward Arnold, 1906), 165.
5. Stan Larson, "The King Follett Discourse: A Newly Amalgamated Text," *BYU Studies* 18, no. 2 (Winter 1978): 203–4.
6. C. S. Lewis, *Perelandra* (New York: Scribner, 1996), 142.
7. Nikolai Berdyaev, *The Destiny of Man* (London: Geoffrey Bles, 1937), 190.
8. Parley P. Pratt, *The Millennium, and Other Poems: To Which Is*

Annexed, A Treatise on the Regeneration and Eternal Duration of Matter (New York: Molineux, 1840), 110.
9. David L. Paulsen, cited in *Mormonism at the Crossroads of Philosophy and Theology: Essays in Honor of David L. Paulsen*, ed. Jacob T. Baker (Salt Lake City: Kofford, 2012), xxxix.
10. Richard Dawkins, *The God Delusion* (New York: Houghton Mifflin, 2008), 52.
11. "Richard Dawkins Explains 'The God Delusion,'" *Fresh Air with Terry Gross*, March 28, 2007, http://www.npr.org/templates/story/story.php?storyId=9180871.
12. Larson, "King Follett Discourse," 201.
13. John A. Widtsoe, *A Rational Theology* (Salt Lake City: Mutual Improvement Association, 1915), 23–24.
14. "The Origin of Man," *Ensign*, February 2002, https://www.churchofjesuschrist.org/study/ensign/2002/02/the-origin-of-man?lang=eng.
15. Elizabeth Cady Stanton, *The Woman's Bible* (New York: Prometheus Books, 1999). For a discussion of Stanton and Latter-day Saint theology, see Fiona Givens, "Feminism and Heavenly Mother," *Routledge Handbook of Mormonism and Gender* (Abingdon-on-Thames, UK: Routledge, 2020).
16. See "Mother in Heaven," Gospel Topics Essays, The Church of Jesus Christ of Latter-day Saints, https://www.churchofjesuschrist.org/study/manual/gospel-topics-essays/mother-in-heaven?lang=eng; emphasis added.
17. Nicholas Wolterstorff, "God Is Everlasting," in *God and the Good: Essays in Honor of Henry Stob*, ed. Clifton Orlebeke and Lewis Smedes (Grand Rapids, MI: Eerdmans, 1975), 197.

Chapter 5: The Stories We Tell

1. An extensive literature discusses the "zombie problem" and how we cannot know, but operate on, the assumption that other humans are conscious agents like ourselves.
2. Annaka Harris, *Conscious: A Brief Guide to the Fundamental Mystery of the Mind* (New York: Harper 2019), 21.
3. Jeffrey R. Holland, "Who We Are and What God Expects Us to Do," September 15, 1987, BYU Speeches, https://speeches.byu.edu/talks/jeffrey-r-holland/god-expects-us/.
4. The term *passions* has a complex theological and philosophical history: most Christian treatments before the twentieth century, however, emphasized that God is not "moved" by the suffering of another. Neither "the needs" nor "the claims of his creation," nor "pity," can act upon Him from without. "His will is determined from within," as one defense of the doctrine explains. G. L. Prestige, *God in Patristic Thought* (Eugene, OR: Wipf and Stock, 2008), 6–7.
5. This purpose behind human creation has been affirmed consistently throughout Christian history. See Tertullian, *The Writings*, ed. Anthony Uyl (Ontario, Canada: Devoted Publishing, 2017), 1:36;

NOTES

Thomas Watson, "Man's Chief End Is to Glorify God," in *A Body of Practical Divinity* (Philadelphia: T. Wardle, 1833), 8; Roger E. Olson, *The Story of Christian Theology* (Downers Grove, IL: InterVarsity Press, 1999), 506; *The Catechism of Christian Doctrine: Prepared and Enjoined by Order of the Third Plenary Council of Baltimore* (Philadelphia: Cunningham and Son, 1885); Rick Warren, *The Purpose Driven Life: What on Earth Am I Here For?* (Grand Rapids, MI: Zondervan, 2012), 53; John Piper, *The Pleasures of God* (Colorado Springs: Multnomah Books, 2012), 29, 192.

6. Frank Wilczek, *Fundamentals: Ten Keys to Reality* (New York: Penguin, 2021), 63. Wilczek writes this approximately 2,500 years after Heraclitus, one of the earliest of Western philosophers, taught that all things are in constant flux.

7. William Herschel, "On the Construction of the Heavens," *Philosophical Transactions of the Royal Society of London* 75 (1785): 216.

8. Richard Holmes, *The Age of Wonder: How the Romantic Generation Discovered the Beauty and Terror of Science* (London: HarperCollins, 2008), 191–92.

9. Alan Lightman, *Probable Impossibilities* (New York: Pantheon Books, 2021), 20.

10. Stan Larson, "The King Follett Discourse: A Newly Amalgamated Text," *BYU Studies* 18, no. 2 (Winter 1978): 204.

11. *The Complete Discourses of Brigham Young*, ed. Richard S. Van Wagoner (Salt Lake City: Smith-Petit Foundation, 2009), 3:1897.

12. Donald D. Hoffman, *The Case against Reality: Why Evolution Hid the Truth from Our Eyes* (New York: Norton, 2020), 204.

13. Steven Pinker, *Enlightenment Now: The Case for Reason, Science, Humanism, and Progress* (New York: Viking, 2018), cited in Hoffman, *Case against Reality*, 204.

14. Thomas Nagel, *Mind and Cosmos: Why the Materialist Neo-Darwinian Conception of Nature Is Almost Certainly Wrong* (New York: Oxford University Press, 2012), 87.

15. These statements are cited in Christof Koch, *The Feeling of Life Itself: Why Consciousness Is Widespread and Can't Be Computed* (Cambridge, MA: MIT Press, 2020), 3–4.

16. Cited in Michael Brooks, *At the Edge of Uncertainty* (New York: Overlook Press, 2014), 12.

17. Hoffman, *Case against Reality*, 205.

18. George Wald, "Life and Mind in the Universe," in *Cosmos, Bios, Theos*, ed. Henry Margenau and Roy Abraham Vargese (La Salle, IL: Open Court, 1992), 218.

19. We share 99 percent of our DNA with chimps and bonobos. Kate Wong, "Tiny Genetic Differences between Humans and Other Primates Pervade the Genome," *Scientific American*, September 1, 2014, https://www.scientificamerican.com/article/tiny-genetic-differences-between-humans-and-other-primates-pervade-the-genome/.

NOTES

20. Ian Leslie, *Curious: The Desire to Know and Why Your Future Depends on It* (New York: Basic Books, 2014), xx.
21. Leslie, *Curious*, xi.
22. Dieter F. Uchtdorf, "Happiness, Your Heritage," general conference, October 2008, https://www.churchofjesuschrist.org/study/general-conference/2008/10/happiness-your-heritage?lang=eng.
23. Nikolai Berdyaev, *The Destiny of Man* (London: Geoffrey Bles, 1937), 189; emphasis added.
24. Wilczek, *Fundamentals*, 124.
25. Henri Bergson, *The Creative Mind: An Introduction to Metaphysics* (Totowa, NJ: Littlefield, Adams, 1975), 93–94.
26. Max Scheler, *The Human Place in the Cosmos* (Evanston, IL: Northwestern University Press, 2009), 27; emphasis in original.
27. Marilynne Robinson, *What Are We Doing Here?* (New York: Farrar, Straus and Giroux, 2018), 41.
28. Lewis Thomas, "The Wonderful Mistake," in *Being Human: Core Readings in the Humanities*, ed. Leon Kass (New York: Norton, 2004), 32.
29. Robinson, *What Are We Doing Here?* 41.
30. Robinson, *What Are We Doing Here?* 41.
31. Gould, in Thomas, "Wonderful Mistake," 33.
32. Scheler, *Human Place*, 26–27.
33. N. T. Wright, *The Day the Revolution Began: Reconsidering the Meaning of Jesus's Crucifixion* (New York: HarperOne, 2016), 28.
34. Diarmaid MacCulloch, *The Reformation* (New York: Viking, 2004), 730–31.
35. Stuart Squires, *The Pelagian Controversy: An Introduction to the Enemies of Grace* (Eugene, OR: Pickwick, 2019), 191.
36. Elizabeth A. Clark, *The Origenist Controversy: The Cultural Construction of an Early Christian Debate* (Princeton: Princeton University Press, 1992), 250.
37. B. R. Rees, *Pelagius: Life and Letters* (Woodbridge, UK: Boydell Press, 1998), *Letters*, 10.
38. Elaine Pagels, *Adam, Eve, and the Serpent* (New York: Vintage, 1989), 99.
39. D. Todd Christofferson, "Fathers," general conference, April 2016, https://www.churchofjesuschrist.org/study/general-conference/2016/04/fathers?lang=eng.
40. George Q. Cannon, "The Authority to Preach," *Journal of Discourses*, 16:144.
41. Larson, "King Follett Discourse," 204; emphasis added.
42. Larson, "King Follett Discourse," 205.
43. Berdyaev, *Destiny of Man*, 371.
44. *Recognitions of Clement* 1.52, Tertullian, *On the Flesh of Christ* 5, *Ante-Nicene Fathers* [*ANF*], ed. Alexander Roberts and James Donaldson (Peabody, MA: Hendrickson, 1995), 8:91.
45. Berdyaev, *Destiny of Man*, 351.

NOTES

46. E. Brooks Holifield, *Theology in America* (New Haven: Yale University Press, 2003), 335.
47. Stephen Webb, *Jesus Christ, Eternal God: Heavenly Flesh and the Metaphysics of Matter* (New York: Oxford, 2011), 243.

Chapter 6: Scripture

1. Origen, *On First Principles* 4.2.9, trans. John Behr (Oxford: Oxford University Press, 2017), 2:517.
2. Augustine, *Confessions* XI.iii, trans. F. J. Sheed (Indianapolis: Hackett, 1992), 213.
3. Augustine, *On Christian Doctrine* 3.10.14, in Nicene and Post-Nicene Fathers, ed. Philip Schaff (Peabody, MA: Hendrickson, 199), 2:560.
4. Oxford English Dictionary, s.v. "immediately," https://www.oed.com/view/Entry/91839?redirectedFrom=immediately#eid.
5. Frederic William Farrar, *History of Interpretation: Bampton Lectures 1885* (Grand Rapids, MI: Baker Book House, 1961), 329.
6. Westminster Confession, Article I; Jaroslav Pelikan and Valerie Hotchkiss, eds., *Creeds and Confessions of Faith in the Christian Tradition* (New Haven, CT: Yale University Press, 2003), 2:606–8.
7. George Q. Cannon, "The Abundant Testimonies to the Work of God," *Journal of Discourses*, 22:354.
8. See also 1 Chronicles 21:15; Jonah 3:10, NRSV; Matthew 27:5; Acts 1:18; 2 Kings 24:8; 2 Chronicles 36:9.
9. "The Chicago Statement on Biblical Inerrancy," *Themalios* 4, no. 3 (April 1979), https://www.thegospelcoalition.org/themelios/article/the-chicago-statement-on-biblical-inerrancy/.
10. George Q. Cannon, "Spiritual Gifts Attainable," in *Journal of Discourses*, 21:76.
11. "Revelations and Translations: Manuscript Revelation Books (Facsimile Edition)," The Joseph Smith Papers, https://www.josephsmithpapers.org/articles/revelations-manuscript-revelation-books; emphasis added.
12. *The Complete Discourses of Brigham Young*, ed. Richard S. Van Wagoner (Salt Lake City: Smith-Petit Foundation, 2009), 4:2033–34.
13. "Bible, Inerrancy of," Gospel Topics, The Church of Jesus Christ of Latter-day Saints, https://www.churchofjesuschrist.org/study/manual/gospel-topics/bible-inerrancy-of?lang=eng.
14. James Kugel, *How to Read the Bible: A Guide to Scripture Then and Now* (New York: Free Press, 1989), 688–89.
15. Parley P. Pratt, "The Fountain of Knowledge," in *An Appeal to the Inhabitants of the State of New York* (Nauvoo, IL: John Taylor, 1844), 17.
16. *The Words of Joseph Smith*, ed. Andrew F. Ehat and Lyndon W. Cook (Orem, UT: Grandin Book, 1991), 345.
17. Wilford Woodruff, in Conference Report, 1873.
18. Dallin H. Oaks, "Scripture Reading, Revelation, and Joseph Smith's Translation of the Bible," in *Plain and Precious Truths Restored: The*

Doctrinal and Historical Significance of the Joseph Smith Translation, ed. Robert L. Millet and Robert J. Matthews (Salt Lake City: Bookcraft, 1995), 2.
19. Jeffrey R. Holland, "My Words . . . Never Cease," general conference, April 2008, https://www.churchofjesuschrist.org/study/general-conference/2008/04/my-words-never-cease?lang=eng.
20. *Hymns*, no. 175; see Isaiah 53:2.
21. David Bentley Hart, *The New Testament: A Translation* (New Haven: Yale University Press, 2017), xxxii.

Chapter 7: The "New Mormon History"

1. This name was given by many observers to the new, professionalized direction of Latter-day Saint history writing.
2. Following the merger of Lutherans and Reformed Protestants, the old-style Lutherans who resisted the union were imprisoned and suppressed.
3. Will Durant, *The Reformation* (New York: Simon and Schuster, 1957), 490.
4. According to his 1832 account, Joseph was primarily seeking solace and assurance of his personal standing before God. See Karen Lynn Davidson, David J. Whittaker, Mark Ashurst-McGee, and Richard L. Jensen, eds., *Joseph Smith Papers: Histories, Volume 1: Joseph Smith Histories, 1832–1844* (Salt Lake City: Church Historian's Press, 2012), 10–16.
5. Marcellino D'Ambrosio, *When the Church Was Young: Voices of the Early Fathers* (Cincinnati: Servant Books, 2014), 21.
6. Quoted in Rodney Stark, *The Rise of Christianity* (New York: HarperCollins, 1996), 82.
7. Celsus, *On True Doctrine*, trans. and ed. R. Joseph Hoffmann (New York: Oxford University Press, 1987), 75, 102.
8. Tom Holland, *Dominion* (New York: Basic Books, 2021), 493.
9. N. T. Wright, *The Day the Revolution Began: Reconsidering the Meaning of Jesus's Crucifixion* (New York: HarperCollins, 2018), 34.
10. Richard Rohr and Brian D. Mclaren, *The Universal Christ: How a Forgotten Reality Can Change Everything We See, Hope For, and Believe* (New York: Convergent, 2021), 4.
11. David Bentley Hart, "No Turning Back: Peter Sloterdijk's 'After God,'" *Commonweal*, July 14, 2021, https://www.commonwealmagazine.org/no-turning-back-0.
12. *The Complete Discourses of Brigham Young*, ed. Richard S. Van Wagoner (Salt Lake City: Smith-Petit Foundation, 2009), 3:1191.
13. Ann Loades and Robert MacSwain, *The Truth-Seeking Heart: Austin Farrar and His Writings* (Norwich, UK: Canterbury Press, 2006), 197.

NOTES

Chapter 8: The Poverty of Secularism

1. S. M. K. [Sarah M. Kimball], "Plea for the Women of Massachusetts and Mother Eve, vs. Kate Bowers," *Woman's Exponent* 2, no. 18 (February 15, 1874): 141; cited in Boyd J. Petersen, "'Redeemed from the Curse Placed upon Her': Dialogic Discourse on Eve in the Women's Exponent," *Journal of Mormon History* 40, no. 1 (Winter 2014): 155–56. According to John A. Widtsoe, "Each must choose that which concerns the good of others—the greater law—rather than that which chiefly benefits ourselves—the lesser law. . . . That was the choice made in Eden." *Evidences and Reconciliations* (Salt Lake City: Bookcraft, 1947), 2:78.
2. Martin Rees, *Just Six Numbers: The Deep Forces That Shape the Universe* (New York: Basic Books, 2000), 166.
3. The tendency of some modern scientists to veer more toward faith than science has been pointed out by a number of contemporary physicists. See, for instance, Lee Smoli, *The Trouble with Physics: The Rise of String Theory, the Fall of a Science, and What Comes Next* (Boston: Houghton Mifflin, 2007).
4. Anil Ananthaswamy, *Through Two Doors at Once: The Elegant Experiment that Captures the Enigma of Our Quantum Reality* (New York: Penguin, 2018), 226–27.
5. Ananthaswamy, *Through Two Doors at Once*, 227.
6. Ananthaswamy, *Through Two Doors at Once*, 6.
7. Charles Darwin, *Autobiography and Selected Letters* (Mineola, NY: Dover, 1958), 54.
8. George Santayana, *The Sense of Beauty: Being the Outline of Aesthetic Theory* (New York: Dover, 1955), 11.
9. Ralph Waldo Emerson, "Nature," in *Essays*, 2nd ser. (Cambridge, MA: Houghton Mifflin, 1883), 182.
10. V. S. Naipaul, *Guerillas* (New York: Picador, 2011), 22.

Conclusion

1. To be precise, "There is no consistent formal system in which every mathematical truth is provable." Ted Honderich, ed., *The Oxford Companion to Philosophy* (New York: Oxford, 2005), 320.
2. Stephen Budiansky, *Journey to the Edge of Reason: The Life of Kurt Gödel* (New York: Norton, 2021), 278.
3. Os Guinness, "The Meaning of Truth," in *Belief: Readings on the Reason for Faith*, ed. Francis S. Collins (New York: HarperCollins, 2010), 78.
4. Jeffrey R. Holland, "Lord, I Believe," general conference, April 2013, https://www.churchofjesuschrist.org/study/general-conference/2013/04/lord-i-believe?lang=eng.
5. L. Gregory Jones, "Embodying Scripture in the Community of Faith," in *The Art of Reading Scripture*, ed. Ellen F. Davis and Richard B. Hays (Grand Rapids, MI: Eerdmans, 2003), 156.

NOTES

6. Joseph Smith from Liberty Jail to the Church at Quincy, Illinois, March 20, 1839, in *Personal Writings of Joseph Smith*, rev. ed., ed. Dean C. Jessee (Salt Lake City: Deseret Book, 2002), 436.
7. Cited in Michael Strevens, *The Knowledge Machine: How Irrationality Created Modern Science* (New York: Liveright, 2020), 290.
8. Julian of Norwich, *Revelations of Divine Love*, trans. Barry Windeatt (Oxford: Oxford University Press, 2015), 48.
9. Charles Beecher, "Biography of Edward Beecher," unpublished typescript in author's possession. The book he produced—a defense of human preexistence called *Conflict of the Ages: Or The Great Debate on the Moral Relations of God and Man* (Boston: Phillips, Sampson & Company, 1853)—cost him a brilliant future in American theology.
10. Marilynne Robinson, *What Are We Doing Here?* (New York: Farrar, Straus and Giroux, 2018), 36.
11. Druin Burch, *The Shape of Things to Come* (London: Head of Zeus, 2019), 200.
12. Sam Chambers, "Bloomberg: War on Smoking," University of Washington, July 6, 2015, https://globalhealth.washington.edu/news/2015/07/06/bloomberg-war-smoking#:~:text=In%20the%2020th%20century%20tobacco,they%20were%20doing%20to%20themselves.
13. Joseph Henrich, *The WEIRDest People in the World: How the West Became Psychologically Peculiar and Particularly Prosperous* (New York: Farrar, Straus and Giroux, 2020), 5.
14. Agnes Callard, *Aspiration: The Agency of Becoming* (New York: Oxford University Press, 2018), 1–2.
15. Johann Gottlieb Fichte, *The Vocation of Man*, in *The Popular Works of Johann Gottlieb Fichte* (London: Trubner, 1889), 156.
16. Dean Buonomano, *Brain Bugs: How the Brain's Flaws Shape Our Lives* (New York: Norton, 2011), 199.
17. Diana Butler Bass, *A People's History of Christianity* (New York: HarperCollins, 2005), 60.
18. Her words, reported widely secondhand, cannot be traced to an original source. If the report is apocryphal, the point is indisputably true. Ancient peoples cared for the infirm.
19. Bertrand Russell, *The Conquest of Happiness* (London: George Allen and Unwin, 1996), 111.
20. Cited in Lee G. Bolman and Joan V. Gallos, *Engagement* (Hoboken, NJ: Wiley and Sons, 2016), 131.
21. Fyodor Dostoevsky to N. D. Fonvizina, cited in Richard Pevear, introduction to Fyodor Doestoevsky, *The Brothers Karamazov*, trans. Richard Pevear and Larissa Volokhonsky (New York: Picador, 2021), xv.

Epilogue

Chapter epigraph: "Discourse, 16 June 1844–A, as Reported by Thomas Bullock," [2], The Joseph Smith Papers, accessed February 11,

NOTES

2022, https://www.josephsmithpapers.org/paper-summary/discourse-16-june-1844-a-as-reported-by-thomas-bullock/2.

1. "On the pedestal, these words appear: / My name is Ozymandias, King of Kings; / Look on my Works, ye Mighty, and despair! / Nothing beside remains." Percy Bysshe Shelly, "Ozymandias," *The Norton Anthology of English Literature: The Romantic Period*, 10th ed., vol. D, ed. Stephen Greenblatt (New York: Norton, 2018). 790–91.
2. George Herbert, "Church Monuments," in *The Temple and Other English Poems* (Oxford: University of Oxford, 1883), 58.
3. Austin Farrer, *The Truth-Seeking Heart: Austin Farrer and His Writings*, ed. Ann Loades and Robert MacSwain (Atlanta: Canterbury Press, 2006). The ice-pick phrase is from Franz Kafka in a letter to Oskar Pollak, January 27, 1904, in *Letters to Friends, Family and Editors*, trans. Richard Winston and Clara Winston (New York: Schocken, 1990), 16.
4. John Dewey, *A Common Faith* (New Haven: Yale University Press 1934), 19.
5. Robert Frost, "On the Poet Amy Lowell," *The Christian Science Monitor*, May 16, 1925, https://www.csmonitor.com/The-Culture/Poetry/2013/0430/Robert-Frost-on-poet-Amy-Lowell.
6. William Wordsworth, "Ode: Intimations of Immortality," in *Poetical Works* (Oxford: Oxford University Press, 1989), 461.

INDEX

Abbey of St Albans, 28–29
Abduction, 55
Abelard, Pierre, 27–28
Abundant life, 104
Agency, 50, 67, 105
d'Ailly, Pierre, 25
Alter, Robert, 18
Andersen, Neil L., 47
Anti-intellectualism, 18, 22, 47
Aristotle, 7, 19–20
Arulenus Rusticus, 22
Atheism, 1, 96–97, 114n3
Augustine of Hippo, 67, 71, 73
Auschwitz, 48

Ballard, M. Russell, 47
Beautiful, and choosing belief system, 95–97
Beecher, Edward, 101–2, 127n9
Belief, 100
Belief system, choosing, 95–97
Bennion, Lowell, 7
Berdyaev, Nikolai, 50, 63, 68
Bergson, Henri, 64
Bible: contradictions in, 73–74; errors in, 74–75, 80–81; translation and transmission of, 74–75; hardness of language in, 78–79; and Restoration, 85; and rise of Protestantism, 85
Biblical Christianity, crisis in, 70–71
Biblical interpretation: background on, 71–73; Latter-day Saint, 73–82

Books, early Saints' taste in, 41
Boredom, 65
Brigham Young Academy, 45, 46*f*
Brigham Young University, 45
Burch, Druin, 104

Calvin, John, 85
Cannon, George Q., 67, 73, 74–75
Cathedral schools, 27
Catholicism, 84–85
Celsus, 117n13
Chalmers, David, 61–62
Change, 57–60, 104–5
Chesterton, G. K., 9
"Chicago Statement in Biblical Inerrancy," 74
Christianity: reason and early, 17–23; inquisitions and intellect in history of, 24–30; re-examination of alternative views of future, 66; central elements disappeared from, 66–67; crisis in biblical, 70–71; Restoration and fragmentation of, 85–86; understanding of love in, 88–89
Christofferson, D. Todd, 67
Church of Jesus Christ of Latter-day Saints, The: education and religiosity of members of, 2; value of knowledge, 36, 38; and education of women, 39–40; intellectual engagement with doctrine and history of, 47; "New Mormon history," 84–91

INDEX

Circumcision, for Gentile converts in New Testament church, 86–87
Clarke, Elizabeth, 67
Clement of Alexandria, 21–22
Cole, Adelia, 40
Cole, Joseph, 40
Columbus, Christopher, 25
Compassion, 52–53, 105–6
Consciousness, 55, 61–62
Contradictions, in Bible, 73–74
Cook, Quentin L., 1
Copernicus, Nicholas, 25
Coray, Harold, 40
Coray, Martha, 40
Cosmic observations, 10–12
Cowdery, Oliver, 38
Creation: understanding, 10–12; as ongoing, 58–59; and creativity, 63; dating, 73
Creativity, 63
Crosby, Caroline, 39
Culture, power of, 103–5
Curiosity, 7–8, 10–12, 62–63, 106
Cyprian of Carthage, 105–6

D'Ambrosio, Marcelo, 88
Damnation, 35
Dark Ages. *See* Middle Ages
Darwin, Charles, 95–96
Dawkins, Richard, 53, 114n3
Dead, salvation of, 68
Dennett, Daniel, 61
Descartes, Rene, 25
Dick, Thomas, 34–35
Discipleship, as costly, 82–83, 102
Disease, 50
DNA, 62, 64–65
Dostoevsky, Fyodor, 107
Doubt, 1, 114n3. *See also* Atheism
Draper, John, 24–25

Eagleton, Terry, 114n3
Earth, curiosity and understanding regarding, 10–12. *See also* Creation
Education: faith and, 1–2; as principle of Zion and salvation, 33–35; and School of the Prophets, 35–38; and Hebrew School, 38; of Joseph Smith's inner circle, 38–39; of Latter-day Saint women, 39–40, 43–44; and University of Nauvoo, 40–41; and early Saints' taste in books, 41; premigration gathering of educational materials, 41–42; and intellectual societies in Salt Lake Valley, 42–43; and schools in Utah, 45; and joy in pursuit of knowledge, 45–46; and intellectual engagement with Church doctrine and history, 47
Efficiency, 5–6
Einstein, Albert, 12, 58, 98, 106
Emerson, Ralph Waldo, 96
Enlightenment, 70
Error, 64–65
Eve, 54, 92
Evil, problem of God and, 48–54, 121n4
Exaltation, 53

Faith: persistence of, 1–2; and intellect, 2–3, 8–10, 18–19; reflective, 3–4; and reason, 20–23; and intellectual engagement with Church doctrine and history, 47; in God, 52; defined, 56; Restoration conception of, 68–69
Fall of Adam, 54, 92
Farrer, Austin, 91
Feyerabend, Paul, 25
Fichte, Johann Gottlieb, 105
Fideists, 21
Frost, Robert, 110

Galileo, 24, 25, 101
Gentile converts, circumcision of, in New Testament church, 86–87

INDEX

Geological science, 71
Gilson, Étienne, 21
Gleiser, Marcelo, 11
Glory, intelligence as, 56
God: and humans' learning, 12; love of, 18, 88–89; and explaining evil and suffering, 48–54, 121n4; glory of, 56; and ongoing Creation, 58–59; and spiritual progression, 59; language used by, 78–79; as living, speaking God, 81–82; reality of, 91; learning things of, 100–101
Gödel, Kurt, 98–99
Good, and choosing belief system, 96–97
Gould, Jay, 20, 65

Haidt, Jonathan, 4
Hart, David Bentley, 28, 29, 82, 89
Heaven, 53–54
Hebrew School, 38, 39
Herrad, abbess of Hohenberg, 29
Herschel, William, 57–58
Hoffman, Donald, 61, 62
Holland, Jeffrey R., 56, 81, 100
Holland, Tom, 89
Holocaust, 48
Holy Ghost, 81–82
Holy of Holies, 80
Human life, explaining, in universe, 92–94
Human nature and identity, 4–8, 49–50, 55, 65–66, 67–68
Humans: unique intelligence of, 62–64; capacity for error, 64–65; purpose of, 104, 105
Hyde, Orson, 38

Illness, 50
Incompleteness theorem, 98–99
Inference, 55–56
Infinite universes, 93–94
Intellect, faith and, 2–3, 8–10, 18–19

Intelligence: as glory, 56; as eternal, 59; as foundational to meaningful existence, 60–66; Restoration teachings on, 67–68; and spiritual progression, 106
Intuition, 99

Jackson County, Missouri, 33–34
Jesus Christ: resurrection of, 2–3, 19–20, 87; questions regarding, 87, 90; salvific reality of, 90–91
Job, 17–18, 116n2
Johnson, Samuel, 6
Journey, focusing on, 5
Joy, in pursuit of knowledge, 45–46
Judge, Edwin, 28
Julian of Norwich, 101
Justin Martyr, 21

Kanzi (chimpanzee), 62
Kepler, Johannes, 25
Kimball, Sarah, 39
Kimball, Spencer W., 45
Kindness, 99
Kirtland School of the Prophets, 35–36, 37f
Knowledge, 8–9; as principle of Zion and salvation, 33–35; and School of the Prophets, 35–38; and Hebrew School, 38; of Joseph Smith's inner circle, 38–39; and education of Latter-day Saint women, 39–40, 43–44; and University of Nauvoo, 40–41; and early Saints' taste in books, 41; and premigration gathering of educational materials, 41–42; and intellectual societies in Salt Lake Valley, 42–43; and schools in Utah, 45; joy in pursuit of, 45–46; and intellectual engagement with Church doctrine and history,

INDEX

47; and spiritual progression, 106. *See also* Learning
Krauss, Lawrence, 11

Language, 62–63; scriptural, 78–80
Learning: pursuit of, 7; and cosmic observations, 10–12; interconnection of religion and, 18; transformation through, 63–64. *See also* Knowledge
Leslie, Ian, 62
Levi, Primo, 48
Lewis, C. S., 28, 50
Lightfoot, John, 73
Love: need for, 6–7; of God, 18, 88–89
Luther, Martin, 72–73, 85
Lyell, Charles, 71

"Many world" interpretation of quantum physics, 94
Maslow, Abraham, 4–5, 8, 65
Maxwell, Neal A., 13
McGrath, Alister, 114n3
McLaren, Brian, 89
McLellin, William E., 38
Mead, Margaret, 106
Meaningful existence, 60–66
Medical education, of women, 44
Merton, Thomas, 5
Middle Ages, 24–30
Milky Way galaxy, 11
Milton, John, 10
Monasteries, 28–29
Monks, 28–29
"Mormon history, new," 84–91
Multiverse, infinite, 93–94
Myths, 19–23

Nagel, Thomas, 61
Naipaul, V. S., 97
Natural laws, 51, 53, 57–58
Nelson, Russell M., 47
Nero, 22
"New Mormon history," 84–91
Newton, Isaac, 25
Nibley, Hugh, 5–6

Noll, Mark, 25
Numbers, Ronald, 25

Oaks, Dallin H., 81
Observatory, of Orson Pratt, 43, 44f
Origen of Alexandria, 22–23, 67, 71, 73
Original sin, 66–67
Others, self-awareness of, 55
Ozymandias, 109, 128n1

Pagels, Elaine, 67
Paulsen, David L., 52
Pelagius, 66–67
Perfection, 105
Personal growth, 104–5
Pheasants, breeding of, 104
Phelps, William Wines, 40–41
Philo of Alexandria, 71, 73
Philosophy, 21–22
Physical laws, 51, 53, 57–58
Pinker, Steven, 61
Plague of Galen (165–180), 105–6
Polysophical Society, 42–43
Pratt, Orson, 37, 40–41, 43
Pratt, Parley P., 36, 51, 81
Preconceptions, power of, 103–4
Premack, David, 5
Premortal existence, 102
Presentism, 78–79
Protestantism, rise of, 85
Protestant Reformation, 72–73
Putnam, George, 26–27

Rationality, 105
Reason: faith and, 2–3, 8–10, 20–23; and Christian beginnings, 17–23
Rees, Martin, 93
Reformation, 72–73
Religion: interconnection of learning and, 18; science and, 20–21, 24–30; criticism of, 100
Religiosity, in American culture, 1–2
Restoration, 68–69, 85, 89–91

INDEX

Restoration narrative, 56–57, 87–88

Resurrection, 2–3, 19–20, 87

Revelation: imperfect, 75–78; scripture versus, 81–82

"Revelation books," of Joseph Smith, 75, 76–77f

Rigdon, Sidney, 38, 40

Righteousness, 116n2

Roberts, B. H., 43

Robinson, Marilynne, 64, 65, 103

Rohr, Richard, 89

Rome, 22, 105

Russell, Bertrand, 106

Salvation: knowledge as principle of, 34–35; and original sin, 66–67; and vicarious ordinances for dead, 68; Restoration and reality of, 90–91

Santayana, George, 96

Scheler, Max, 64, 65–66

Schleiermacher, Friedrich, 23

Scholarship, tenacity in, 102–3, 106–7

School of the Prophets, 35–36, 37f

Schools, cathedral, 27

Science: faith and, 1–2; religion and, 20–21, 24–30; as truth, 37; and physical laws, 51, 53; geological, 71

Scripture: and crisis in biblical Christianity, 70–71; background on scriptural interpretation, 71–73; Latter-day Saint scriptural interpretation, 73–82; and costly discipleship, 82–83; and Restoration, 85; and rise of Protestantism, 85

Searle, John, 61

Secularism, 70, 92–97

Self-actualization, 4–5

Self-awareness, of other people, 55

Selfishness, 49

Shelley, Percy Bysshe, 109, 128n1

Sin, natural inclination toward, 49

Smith, Joseph: and knowledge as principle of salvation, 33–35; and School of the Prophets, 35–36, 37–38; and Hebrew School, 38; educational backgrounds of associates of, 38–39; and University of Nauvoo, 40; on God's nature, 49; on intelligence, 59; on spiritual progression, 68; "revelation books" of, 75, 76–77f; on scripture versus revelation, 81; in Latter-day Saint history, 84, 86; and Restoration, 85–86, 89–90; on things of God, 100–101

Snow, Eliza R., 39, 40, 44

Snow, Lorenzo, 39, 42–43

Solar eclipses, 10–11

Souls, eternal, 59–60

Spencer, Orson, 40

Spirituality, 97

Spiritual progression, 53, 59–60, 68, 106

Stanton, Elizabeth Cady, 54

Stoppard, Tom, 6–7

Straw men arguments, 17–23

Strawson, Galen, 61

Subatomic behavior, 94, 95

Suffering: of Job, 17–18; problem of God and, 48–54, 121n4

Taylor, Charles, 8

Taylor, John, 30

Temple work, 68

Tertullian, 17, 19–20

Thomas, Lewis, 64

Thorp, Judge, 39–40

Titus, 22

Trust, in God, 52

Truth: eternal nature of, 36–37; scriptural, 73; and choosing belief system, 95, 96–97; and incompleteness theorem, 98–99; importance of, 99–100

INDEX

Uchtdorf, Dieter F., 63
Understanding: regarding Creation, 10–12; Job's quest for, 17–18, 116n2
Universal laws, 51, 53, 57–58
Universal Scientific Society, 43
Universe(s): expansion of, 58–59; infinite, 93–94; complexity of, 94–95
Universities, 27–28
University of Nauvoo, 40–41
Ussher, James, 73

Vespasian, 22

Wald, George, 62
Webb, Stephen, 69
Wesley, John, 85
Westminster Confession, 72–73
White, A. D., 24–25
Widtsoe, John, 53, 126n1
Wilczek, Frank, 57, 64
Wilson, E. O., 5
Wirthlin, Joseph B., 13
Wolterstorff, Nicholas, 54
Women, education of Latter-day Saint, 39–40, 43–44
Woodruff, Wilford, 39, 43, 81
Wordsworth, William, 5, 110
Wright, N. T., 89

Young, Brigham: on salvation, 35; on knowledge, 36; encourages Saints to gather educational materials, 41–42; on education of women, 44; establishes Latter-day Saint academies, 45; on joy in pursuit of knowledge, 45–46; on spiritual progression, 59–60; on scriptural language, 79; on Restoration doctrine, 90
Young Men's Club of Centerville, Utah, 43

Zion, knowledge as principle of, 33–47